TELEPORTATION

THE DREAM OF INSTANT TRANSLOCATION MOVES FROM THE HOLLYWOOD SOUNDSTAGE TO SECRET U. S. AIRFORCE LABORATORIES

SECRET
GOVERNMENT
RESEARCH
REVEALED!

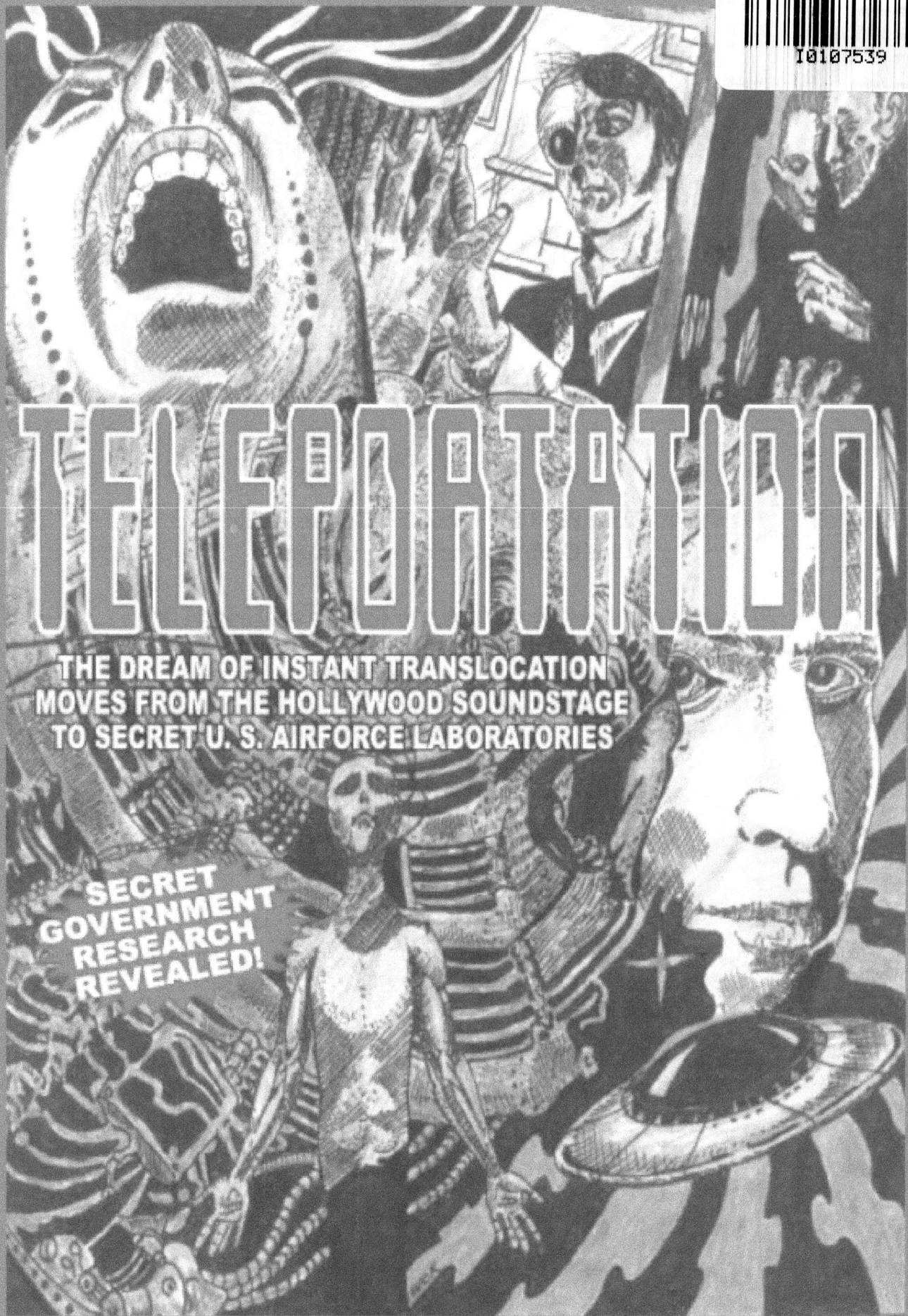

Teleportation

The Dream Of Instant Translocation Moves From The Hollywwood Sound Stage To Secret U. S. Air Force Laboratories
Special Limited Edition
Special Reprint

Eric Davis

© 2007 and 2013 by Timothy Green Beckley
dba Global Communications

ISBN: 1606111485
ISBN 13: 9781606111482

Global Communications / Inner Light
Box 753 · New Brunswick, NJ 08903

GLOBAL COMMUNICATIONS
EX LIBRIS

POST OFFICE BOX 753
NEW BRUNSWICK, NJ 08903

Free weekly newsletter at:
www.ConspiracyJournal.com

AFRL-PR-ED-TR-2003-0034   AFRL-PR-ED-TR-2003-0034

Teleportation Physics Study

Eric W. Davis
Warp Drive Metrics
4849 San Rafael Ave.
Las Vegas, NV 89120

August 2004

Special Report

APPROVED FOR PUBLIC RELEASE; DISTRIBUTION UNLIMITED.

AIR FORCE RESEARCH LABORATORY
AIR FORCE MATERIEL COMMAND
EDWARDS AIR FORCE BASE CA 93524-7048

1. REPORT DATE (DD-MM-YYYY) 25-11-2003	2. REPORT TYPE Special	3. DATES COVERED (From - To) 30 Jan 2001 – 28 Jul 2003	
4. TITLE AND SUBTITLE **Teleportation Physics Study**		**5a. CONTRACT NUMBER** F04611-99-C-0025	
		5b. GRANT NUMBER	
		5c. PROGRAM ELEMENT NUMBER 62500F	
6. AUTHOR(S) Eric W. Davis		**5d. PROJECT NUMBER** 4847	
		5e. TASK NUMBER 0159	
		5f. WORK UNIT NUMBER 549907	
7. PERFORMING ORGANIZATION NAME(S) AND ADDRESS(ES) Warp Drive Metrics 4849 San Rafael Ave. Las Vegas, NV 89120		**8. PERFORMING ORGANIZATION REPORT NO.**	
9. SPONSORING / MONITORING AGENCY NAME(S) AND ADDRESS(ES) Air Force Research Laboratory (AFMC) AFRL/PRSP 10 E. Saturn Blvd. Edwards AFB CA 93524-7680		**10. SPONSOR/MONITOR'S ACRONYM(S)**	
		11. SPONSOR/MONITOR'S REPORT NUMBER(S) **AFRL-PR-ED-TR-2003-0034**	

12. DISTRIBUTION / AVAILABILITY STATEMENT

Approved for public release; distribution unlimited.

13. SUPPLEMENTARY NOTES

14. ABSTRACT

This study was tasked with the purpose of collecting information describing the teleportation of material objects, providing a description of teleportation as it occurs in physics, its theoretical and experimental status, and a projection of potential applications. The study also consisted of a search for teleportation phenomena occurring naturally or under laboratory conditions that can be assembled into a model describing the conditions required to accomplish the transfer of objects. This included a review and documentation of quantum teleportation, its theoretical basis, technological development, and its potential applications. The characteristics of teleportation were defined and physical theories were evaluated in terms of their ability to completely describe the phenomena. Contemporary physics, as well as theories that presently challenge the current physics paradigm were investigated. The author identified and proposed two unique physics models for teleportation that are based on the manipulation of either the general relativistic spacetime metric or the spacetime vacuum electromagnetic (zero-point fluctuations) parameters. Naturally occurring anomalous teleportation phenomena that were previously studied by the United States and foreign governments were also documented in the study and are reviewed in the report. The author proposes an additional model for teleportation that is based on a combination of the experimental results from the previous government studies and advanced physics concepts. Numerous recommendations outlining proposals for further theoretical and experimental studies are given in the report. The report also includes an extensive teleportation bibliography.

15. SUBJECT TERMS

teleportation; physics, quantum teleportation; teleportation phenomena; anomalous teleportation; teleportation theories; teleportation experiments; teleportation bibliography

16. SECURITY CLASSIFICATION OF:			17. LIMITATION OF ABSTRACT	18. NUMBER OF PAGES	19a. NAME OF RESPONSIBLE PERSON Franklin B. Mead, Jr.
a. REPORT Unclassified	**b. ABSTRACT** Unclassified	**c. THIS PAGE** Unclassified	A	88	**19b. TELEPHONE NO** (include area code) (661) 275-5929

NOTICE

USING GOVERNMENT DRAWINGS, SPECIFICATIONS, OR OTHER DATA INCLUDED IN THIS DOCUMENT FOR ANY PURPOSE OTHER THAN GOVERNMENT PROCUREMENT DOES NOT IN ANY WAY OBLIGATE THE US GOVERNMENT. THE FACT THAT THE GOVERNMENT FORMULATED OR SUPPLIED THE DRAWINGS, SPECIFICATIONS, OR OTHER DATA DOES NOT LICENSE THE HOLDER OR ANY OTHER PERSON OR CORPORATION; OR CONVEY ANY RIGHTS OR PERMISSION TO MANUFACTURE, USE, OR SELL ANY PATENTED INVENTION THAT MAY RELATE TO THEM.

FOREWORD

This Special Technical Report presents the results of a subcontracted study performed by Warp Drive Metrics, Las Vegas, NV, under Contract No. F04611-99-C-0025, for the Air Force Research Laboratory (AFRL)/Space and Missile Propulsion Division, Propellant Branch (PRSP), Edwards AFB, CA. The Project Manager for AFRL/PRSP was Dr. Franklin B. Mead, Jr.

This report has been reviewed and is approved for release and distribution in accordance with the distribution statement on the cover and on the SF Form 298. This report is published in the interest of scientific and technical information exchange and does not constitute approval or disapproval of its ideas or findings.

//Signed//   //Signed//
_____   _____
FRANKLIN B. MEAD, JR.   RONALD E. CHANNELL
Project Manager   Chief, Propellants Branch

//Signed//   //Signed//   AFRL-ERS-PAS-04-155
_____   _____
PHILIP A. KESSEL   RANNEY G. ADAMS III
Technical Advisor, Space and Missile   Public Affairs Director
Propulsion Division

Table of Contents

List of Figures

List of Tables

Glossary

AEC   Average Energy Condition
AFRL   Air Force Research Laboratory
AU   Astronomical Unit
BBO   Beta (β)-Barium Borate
CGS   Centimeter-Gram-Second
CIA   Central Intelligence Agency
DARPA   Defense Advanced Research Projects Agency
DEC   Dominant Energy Condition
DIA   Defense Intelligence Agency
DNA   Deoxyribo Nucleic Acid
DoD   Department of Defense
EPR   Einstein, Podolsky and Rosen
ESP   Extrasensory Perception
eV   Electron Volt
FRW   Friedmann-Robertson-Walker
FTL   Faster-Than-Light
IBM   International Business Machines
INSCOM   Intelligence and Security Command
IR   Infrared
MeV   Mega-Electron Volt
MKS   Meter-Kilogram-Second
NEC   Null Energy Condition
NLP   Neuro-Linguistic Programming
NMR   Nuclear Magnetic Resonance
NSA   National Security Agency
PK   Psychokinesis
PPN   Parameterized Post-Newtonian
PRC   Peoples Republic of China
PV-GR   Polarizable-Vacuum Representation of General Relativity
QED   Quantum Electrodynamics
QISP   Quantum Information Science Program
R&D   Research and Development
SAIC   Science Applications International Corporation
SEC   Strong Energy Condition
SRI   Stanford Research Institute
USSR   Union of Soviet Socialist Republics
UV   Ultraviolet
WEC   Weak Energy Condition
ZPE   Zero-Point Energy
ZPF   Zero-Point Fluctuations

Acknowledgements

This study would not have been possible without the very generous support of Dr. Frank Mead, Senior Scientist at the Advanced Concepts Office of the U.S. Air Force Research Laboratory (AFRL) Propulsion Directorate at Edwards AFB, CA. Dr. Mead's collegial collaboration, ready assistance, and constant encouragement were invaluable to me. Dr. Mead's professionalism and excellent rapport with "out-of-the-box" thinkers excites and motivates serious exploration into advanced concepts that push the envelope of knowledge and discovery. The author owes a very large debt of gratitude and appreciation to both Dr. David Campbell, Program Manager, ERC, Inc. at AFRL, Edwards AFB, CA, and the ERC, Inc. staff, for supporting the project contract and for making all the paperwork fuss totally painless. Dr. Campbell and his staff provided timely assistance when the author needed it, which helped make this contract project run smoothly.

There are two colleagues who provided important contributions to this study that I wish to acknowledge. First, I would like to express my sincere thanks and deepest appreciation to my first longtime mentor and role model, the late Dr. Robert L. Forward. Bob Forward was the first to influence my interests in interstellar flight and advanced breakthrough physics concepts (i.e., "Future Magic") when I first met him at an AIAA Joint Propulsion Conference in Las Vegas while I was in high school (ca. 1978). The direction I took in life from that point forward followed the trail of exploration and discovery that was blazed by Bob. I will miss him, but I will never forget him. Second, I would like to express my sincere thanks and appreciation to my longtime friend, colleague and present mentor, Dr. Hal Puthoff, Institute for Advanced Studies-Austin, for our many discussions on applying his Polarizable Vacuum-General Relativity model to a quasi-classical teleportation concept. Hal taught me to expand my mind, and he encourages me to think outside the box. He also gave me a great deal of valuable insight and personal knowledge about the Remote Viewing Program. Last, I would like to offer my debt of gratitude and thanks to my business manager (and spouse), Lindsay K. Davis, for all the hard work she does to make the business end of Warp Drive Metrics run smoothly.

Eric W. Davis, Ph.D., FBIS
Warp Drive Metrics
Las Vegas, NV

Preface

The Teleportation Physics Study is divided into four phases. Phase I is a review and documentation of quantum teleportation, its theoretical basis, technological development, and its potential application. Phase II developed a textbook description of teleportation as it occurs in classical physics, explored its theoretical and experimental status, and projected its potential applications. Phase III consisted of a search for teleportation phenomena occurring naturally or under laboratory conditions that can be assembled into a model describing the conditions required to accomplish the disembodied conveyance of objects. The characteristics of teleportation were defined, and physical theories were evaluated in terms of their ability to completely describe the phenomenon. Presently accepted physics theories, as well as theories that challenge the current physics paradigm were investigated for completeness. The theories that provide the best chance of explaining teleportation were selected, and experiments with a high chance of accomplishing teleportation were identified. Phase IV is the final report.

The report contains five chapters. Chapter 1 is an overview of the textbook descriptions for the various teleportation phenomena that are found in nature, in theoretical physics concepts, and in experimental laboratory work. Chapter 2 proposes two quasi-classical physics concepts for teleportation: the first is based on engineering the spacetime metric to induce a traversable wormhole; the second is based on the polarizable-vacuum-general relativity approach that treats spacetime metric changes in terms of equivalent changes in the vacuum permittivity and permeability constants. These concepts are theoretically developed and presented. Promising laboratory experiments were identified and recommended for further research. Chapter 3 presents the current state-of-art of quantum teleportation physics, its theoretical basis, technological development, and its applications. Key theoretical, experimental, and applications breakthroughs were identified, and a series of theoretical and experimental research programs are proposed to solve technical problems and advance quantum teleportation physics. Chapter 4 gives an overview of alternative teleportation concepts that challenge the present physics paradigm. These concepts are based on the existence of parallel universes/spaces and/or extra space dimensions. The theoretical and experimental work that has been done to develop these concepts is reviewed, and a recommendation for further research is made. Last, Chapter 5 gives an in-depth overview of unusual teleportation phenomena that occur naturally and under laboratory conditions. The teleportation phenomenon discussed in the chapter is based on psychokinesis (PK), which is a category of psychotronics. The U.S. military-intelligence literature is reviewed, which relates the historical scientific research performed on PK-teleportation in the U.S., China and the former Soviet Union. The material discussed in the chapter largely challenges the current physics paradigm; however, extensive controlled and repeatable laboratory data exists to suggest that PK-teleportation is quite real and that it is controllable. The report ends with a combined list of references.

TELEPORTATION

1.0 INTRODUCTION

1.1 Introduction

The concept of teleportation was originally developed during the Golden Age of 20th century science fiction literature by writers in need of a form of instantaneous disembodied transportation technology to support the plots of their stories. Teleportation has appeared in such SciFi literature classics as Algis Budry's *Rogue Moon* (Gold Medal Books, 1960), A. E. van Vogt's *World of Null-A* (Astounding Science Fiction, August 1945), and George Langelaan's *The Fly* (Playboy Magazine, June 1957). The Playboy Magazine short story led to a cottage industry of popular films decrying the horrors of scientific technology that exceeded mankind's wisdom: *The Fly* (1958), *Return of the Fly* (1959), *Curse of the Fly* (1965), *The Fly* (a 1986 remake), and *The Fly II* (1989). The teleportation concept has also appeared in episodes of popular television SciFi anthology series such as *The Twilight Zone* and *The Outer Limits*. But the most widely recognized pop-culture awareness of the teleportation concept began with the numerous *Star Trek* television and theatrical movie series of the past 39 years (beginning in 1964 with the first TV series pilot episode, *The Cage*), which are now an international entertainment and product franchise that was originally spawned by the late genius television writer-producer Gene Roddenberry. Because of *Star Trek* everyone in the world is familiar with the "transporter" device, which is used to teleport personnel and material from starship to starship or from ship to planet and vice versa at the speed of light. People or inanimate objects would be positioned on the transporter pad and become completely disintegrated by a beam with their atoms being patterned in a computer buffer and later converted into a beam that is directed toward the destination, and then reintegrated back into their original form (all without error!). *"Beam me up, Scotty"* is a familiar automobile bumper sticker or cry of exasperation that were popularly adopted from the series.

However, the late Dr. Robert L. Forward (2001) stated that modern hard-core SciFi literature, with the exception of the ongoing *Star Trek* franchise, has abandoned using the teleportation concept because writers believe that it has more to do with the realms of parapsychology/paranormal (a.k.a. psychic) and imaginative fantasy than with any realm of science. Beginning in the 1980s developments in quantum theory and general relativity physics have succeeded in pushing the envelope in exploring the reality of teleportation. A crescendo of scientific and popular literature appearing in the 1990s and as recently as 2003 has raised public awareness of the new technological possibilities offered by teleportation. As for the psychic aspect of teleportation, it became known to Dr. Forward and myself, along with several colleagues both inside and outside of government, that anomalous teleportation has been scientifically investigated and separately documented by the Department of Defense.

It has been recognized that extending the present research in quantum teleportation and developing alternative forms of teleportation physics would have a high payoff impact on communications and transportation technologies in the civilian and military sectors. It is the purpose of this study to explore the physics of teleportation and delineate its characteristics and performances, and to make recommendations for further studies in support of Air Force Advanced Concepts programs.

1.2 The Definitions of Teleportation

Before proceeding, it is necessary to give a definition for each of the teleportation concepts I have identified during the course of this study:

TELEPORTATION

> *Teleportation* – SciFi: the disembodied transport of persons or inanimate objects across space by advanced (futuristic) technological means (adapted from Vaidman, 2001). We will call this *sf-Teleportation*, which will not be considered further in this study.

> *Teleportation* – psychic: the conveyance of persons or inanimate objects by psychic means. We will call this *p-Teleportation*.

> *Teleportation* – engineering the vacuum or spacetime metric: the conveyance of persons or inanimate objects across space by altering the properties of the spacetime vacuum, or by altering the spacetime metric (geometry). We will call this *vm-Teleportation*.

> *Teleportation* – quantum entanglement: the disembodied transport of the quantum state of a system and its correlations across space to another system, where *system* refers to any single or collective particles of matter or energy such as baryons (protons, neutrons, etc.), leptons (electrons, etc.), photons, atoms, ions, etc. We will call this *q-Teleportation*.

> *Teleportation* – exotic: the conveyance of persons or inanimate objects by transport through extra space dimensions or parallel universes. We will call this *e-Teleportation*.

We will examine each of these in detail in the following chapters and determine whether any of the above teleportation concepts encompass the instantaneous and or disembodied conveyance of objects through space.

TELEPORTATION

2.0 vm-TELEPORTATION

2.1 Engineering the Spacetime Metric

A comprehensive literature search for vm-Teleportation within the genre of spacetime metric engineering yielded no results. No one in the general relativity community has thought to apply the Einstein field equation to determine whether there are solutions compatible with the concept of teleportation. Therefore, I will offer two solutions that I believe will satisfy the definition of vm-Teleportation. The first solution can be found from the class of traversable wormholes giving rise to what I call a true "stargate." A stargate is essentially a wormhole with a flat-face shape for the throat as opposed to the spherical-shaped throat of the Morris and Thorne (1988) traversable wormhole, which was derived from a spherically symmetric Lorentzian spacetime metric that prescribes the wormhole geometry (see also, Visser, 1995 for a complete review of traversable Lorentzian wormholes):

$$ds^2 = -e^{2\phi(r)}c^2dt^2 + [1-b(r)/r]^{-1}dr^2 + r^2d\Omega^2 \qquad (2.1),$$

where by inspection we can write the traversable wormhole metric tensor in the form

$$g_{\alpha\beta} = \begin{pmatrix} -e^{2\phi(r)} & 0 & 0 & 0 \\ 0 & [1-b(r)/r]^{-1} & 0 & 0 \\ 0 & 0 & r^2 & 0 \\ 0 & 0 & 0 & r^2\sin^2\theta \end{pmatrix} \qquad (2.2)$$

using standard spherical coordinates, where c is the speed of light, $\alpha,\beta \equiv (0 = t, 1 = r, 2 = \theta, 3 = \varphi)$ are the time and space coordinate indices ($-\infty < t < \infty$; r: $2\pi r$ = circumference; $0 \leq \theta \leq \pi$; $0 \leq \varphi \leq 2\pi$), $d\Omega^2 = d\theta^2 + sin^2\theta d\varphi^2$, $\phi(r)$ is the freely specifiable redshift function that defines the proper time lapse through the wormhole throat, and $b(r)$ is the freely specifiable shape function that defines the wormhole throat's spatial (hypersurface) geometry. Such spacetimes are asymptotically flat. The Einstein field equation requires that a localized source of matter-energy be specified in order to determine the geometry that the source induces on the local spacetime. We can also work the Einstein equation backwards by specifying the local geometry in advance and then calculate the matter-energy source required to induce the desired geometry. The Einstein field equation thus relates the spacetime geometry terms comprised of the components of the metric tensor and their derivatives (a.k.a. the Einstein tensor) to the local matter-energy source terms comprised of the energy and stress-tension densities (a.k.a. the stress-energy tensor). The flat-face wormhole or stargate is derived in the following section.

2.1.1 Wormhole Thin Shell Formalism

The flat-face traversable wormhole solution is derived from the thin shell (a.k.a. junction condition or surface layer) formalism of the Einstein equations (Visser, 1989; see also, Misner, Thorne and Wheeler, 1973). We adapt Visser's (1989) development in the following discussion. The procedure is to take two copies of flat Minkowski space and remove from each identical regions of the form $\Omega \times \Re$, where Ω is a three-dimensional compact spacelike hypersurface and $\Re$ is a timelike straight line (time axis). Then identify these two incomplete spacetimes along the timelike boundaries $\partial\Omega \times \Re$. The resulting spacetime

TELEPORTATION

is geodesically complete and possesses two asymptotically flat regions connected by a wormhole. The throat of the wormhole is just the junction $\partial\Omega$ (a two-dimensional space-like hypersurface) at which the two original Minkowski spaces are identified (see Figures 1 and 2).

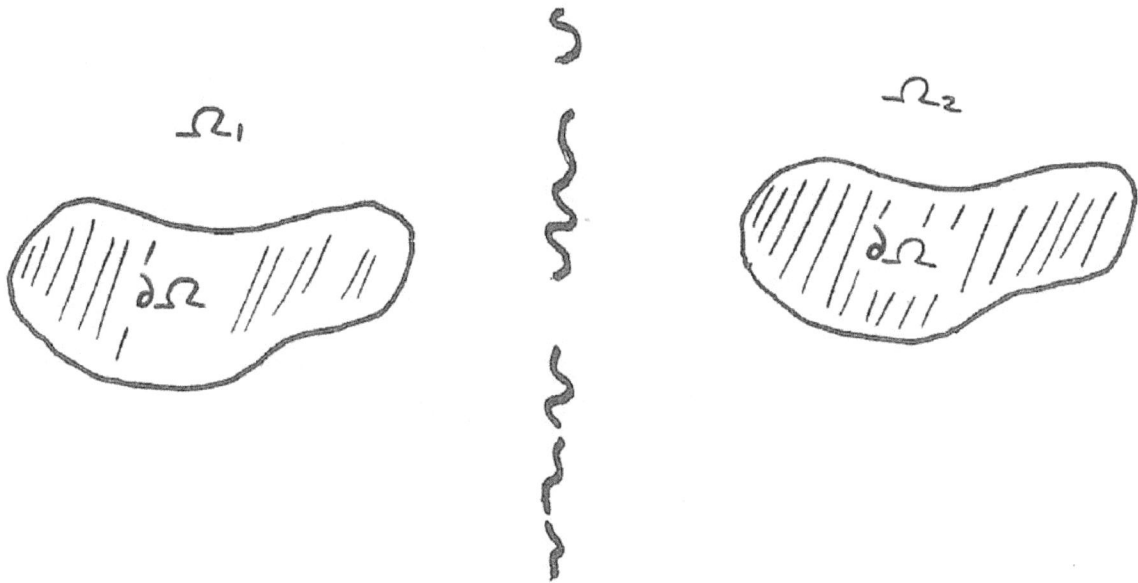

Figure 1. Diagram of a Simultaneous View of Two Remote Compact Regions
(Ω_1 and Ω_2) of Minkowski Space Used to Create the Wormhole Throat $\partial\Omega$,
Where Time is Suppressed in This Representation (adapted from Bennett et al., 1995)

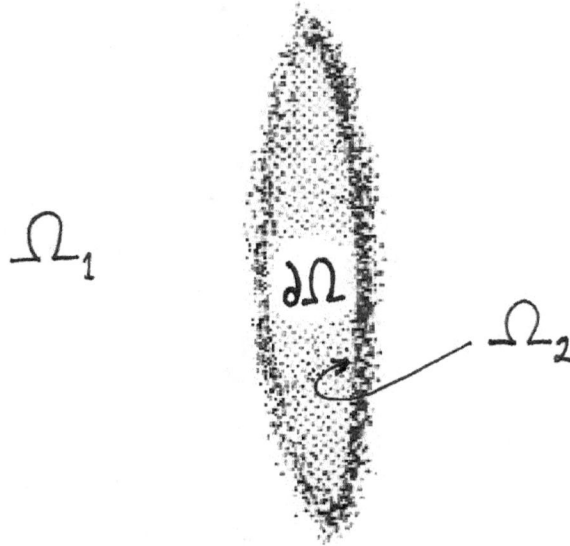

Figure 2. The Same Diagram as in Figure 1 Except as Viewed by an Observer Sitting in Region Ω_1 Who Looks Through the Wormhole Throat $\partial\Omega$ and Sees Remote Region Ω_2 (Dotted Area Inside the Circle) on the Other Side

TELEPORTATION

The resulting spacetime is everywhere Riemann-flat except possibly at the throat. Also, the stress-energy tensor in this spacetime is concentrated at the throat with a δ-function singularity there. This is a consequence of the fact that the spacetime metric at the throat is continuous but not differentiable, while the connection is discontinuous; thus causing the Riemann curvature to possess a δ-function singularity (causing undesirable gravitational tidal forces) there. The magnitude of this δ-function singularity can be calculated in terms of the second fundamental form on both sides of the throat, which we presume to be generated by a localized thin shell of matter-energy. The second fundamental form represents the extrinsic curvature of the $\partial\Omega$ hypersurface (i.e., the wormhole throat), telling how it is curved with respect to the enveloping four-dimensional spacetime. The form of the geometry is simple, so the second fundamental form at the throat is calculated to be (McConnell, 1957):

$$
K^{i}_{\ j}{}^{\pm} = \pm \begin{pmatrix} \kappa_0 & 0 & 0 \\ 0 & \kappa_1 & 0 \\ 0 & 0 & \kappa_2 \end{pmatrix}
$$
$$
= \pm \begin{pmatrix} 0 & 0 & 0 \\ 0 & 1/\rho_1 & 0 \\ 0 & 0 & 1/\rho_2 \end{pmatrix} \qquad (2.3),
$$

where $i,j = 0,1,2$ and $K^{i}_{\ j}{}^{\pm}$ is the second fundamental form. The full 4×4 matrix $K^{\alpha}{}_{\beta}$ has been reduced to 3×3 form, as above, for computational convenience because the thin shell (or hypersurface) is essentially a two-surface embedded in three-space. The overall ± sign in equation (2.3) comes from the fact that a unit normal points outward from one side of the surface and points inward on the other side. We hereafter drop the ± sign for the sake of brevity in notation. The quantities κ_0, κ_1, and κ_2 measure the extrinsic curvature of the thin shell of local matter-energy (i.e., the stuff that induces the wormhole throat geometry). Since the wormhole throat is a space-like hypersurface, we can exclude time-like hypersurfaces and their components in the calculations. Therefore we set $\kappa_0 = 0$ in equation (2.3) because it is the time-like extrinsic curvature for the time-like hypersurface of the thin shell of matter-energy. As seen in equation (2.3) κ_1 and κ_2 are simply related to the two principal radii of curvature ρ_1 and ρ_2 (defined to be the eigenvalues of $K^{i}_{\ j}$) of the two-dimensional spacelike hypersurface $\partial\Omega$ (see Figure 3). It should be noted that a convex surface has positive radii of curvature, while a concave surface has negative radii of curvature.

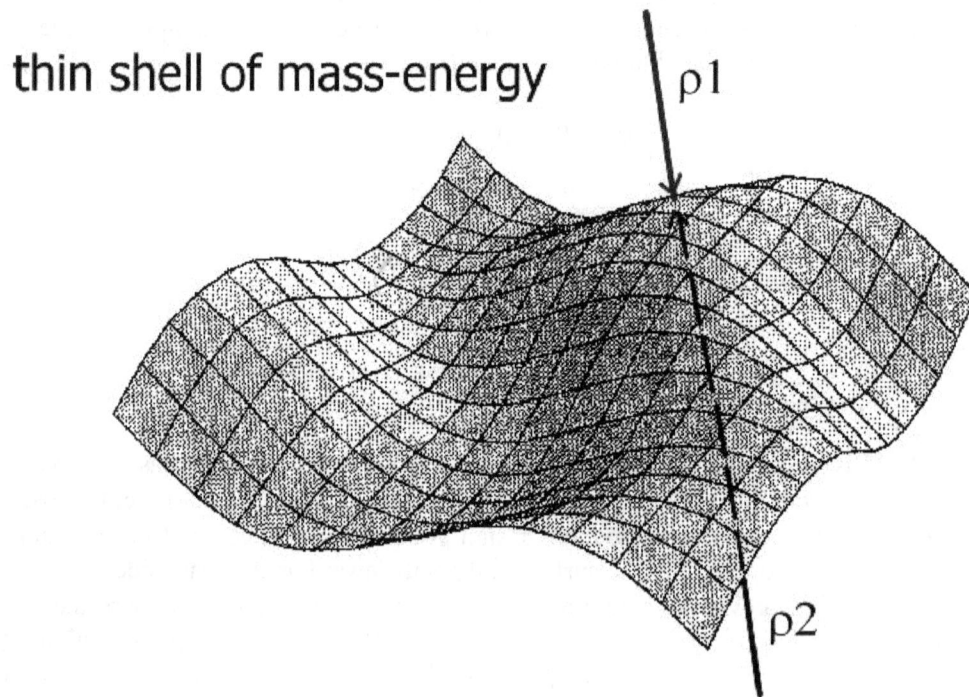

Figure 3. A Thin Shell of (Localized) Matter-Energy, or Rather the Two-Dimensional Spacelike Hypersurface $\partial\Omega$ (via (2.3)), Possessing the Two Principal Radii of Curvature ρ_1 and ρ_2

TELEPORTATION

It is a standard result of the thin shell or junction condition formalism that the Einstein field equation may be cast in terms of the surface stress-energy tensor S^i_j of the thin matter-energy shell localized in $\partial\Omega$ (note: we are exploiting the symmetry of the wormhole with respect to interchange of the two flat regions Ω_1 and Ω_2):

$$S^i_{\,j} = -\frac{c^4}{4\pi G}\left(K^i_{\,j} - \delta^i_{\,j}K^k_{\,k}\right) \quad (2.4),$$

where G is Newton's gravitational constant and $\delta^i_{\,j}$ is the (three-dimensional) unit matrix. $K^k_{\,k}$ is the trace of equation (2.3):

$$
\begin{aligned}
K^k_{\,k} &= Tr\, K^i_{\,j} \\
&= \frac{1}{\rho_1} + \frac{1}{\rho_2} \quad (2.5)
\end{aligned}
$$

and

$$\delta^i_{\,j}K^k_{\,k} = \begin{pmatrix} \dfrac{1}{\rho_1}+\dfrac{1}{\rho_2} & 0 & 0 \\[2mm] 0 & \dfrac{1}{\rho_1}+\dfrac{1}{\rho_2} & 0 \\[2mm] 0 & 0 & \dfrac{1}{\rho_1}+\dfrac{1}{\rho_2} \end{pmatrix} \quad (2.6).$$

Substituting (2.3) and (2.6) into (2.4) gives (after simplification):

$$S^i_{\,j} = \frac{c^4}{4\pi G}\begin{pmatrix} \dfrac{1}{\rho_1}+\dfrac{1}{\rho_2} & 0 & 0 \\[2mm] 0 & 1/\rho_2 & 0 \\[2mm] 0 & 0 & 1/\rho_1 \end{pmatrix} \quad (2.7).$$

The thin matter-energy shell's surface stress-energy tensor may be interpreted in terms of the surface energy density σ and principal surface tensions ϑ_1 and ϑ_2:

$$S^i_{\,j} = \begin{pmatrix} -\sigma & 0 & 0 \\ 0 & -\vartheta_1 & 0 \\ 0 & 0 & -\vartheta_2 \end{pmatrix} \quad (2.8).$$

Thus we arrive at the Einstein field equation by equating (2.8) and (2.7) and multiplying both sides by -1:

TELEPORTATION

$$\begin{pmatrix} \sigma & 0 & 0 \\ 0 & \vartheta_1 & 0 \\ 0 & 0 & \vartheta_2 \end{pmatrix} = -\frac{c^4}{4\pi G} \begin{pmatrix} \dfrac{1}{\rho_1} + \dfrac{1}{\rho_2} & 0 & 0 \\ 0 & 1/\rho_2 & 0 \\ 0 & 0 & 1/\rho_1 \end{pmatrix} \qquad (2.9),$$

which gives the final result

$$\sigma = -\frac{c^4}{4\pi G}\left(\frac{1}{\rho_1} + \frac{1}{\rho_2}\right) \qquad (2.10a)$$

$$\vartheta_1 = -\frac{c^4}{4\pi G}\frac{1}{\rho_2} \qquad (2.10b)$$

$$\vartheta_2 = -\frac{c^4}{4\pi G}\frac{1}{\rho_1} \qquad (2.10c).$$

These are the Einstein equations. Equations (2.10a-c) imply that (for $\partial\Omega$ convex) we are dealing with **_negative_** surface energy density and **_negative_** surface tensions. This result is in fact the primary matter-energy requirement for traversable wormholes, as was proved by Morris and Thorne (1988), and later by Visser (1995), within the paradigm of classical Einstein general relativity. The negative surface tension (= *positive outward pressure*, a.k.a. gravitational repulsion or antigravity) is needed to keep the throat open and stable against collapse. The reader should **not** be alarmed at this result. Negative energies and negative stress-tensions are an acceptable result both mathematically and physically, and they manifest gravitational repulsion (antigravity!) in and around the wormhole throat. One only needs to understand what it means for stress-energy to be negative within the proper context. In general relativity the term "*exotic*" is used in place of "*negative.*" The effects of negative energy have been produced in the laboratory (the Casimir Effect is one example). In short, negative energy arises from Heisenberg's quantum uncertainty principle, which requires that the energy density of any electromagnetic, magnetic, electric or other fields must fluctuate randomly. Even in a vacuum, where the average energy density is zero, the energy density fluctuates. This means that the quantum vacuum can never remain truly empty in the classical sense of the term. The quantum picture of the vacuum is that of a turbulent plenum of virtual (i.e., energy non-conserving) particle pairs that spontaneously pop in and out of existence. The notion of "zero energy" in quantum theory corresponds to the vacuum being filled with such fluctuations going on. This issue is further elaborated on and clarified in greater detail in Appendix A. We will also revisit this in Section 2.2. Finally, it should be noted that for the analysis in this section we assumed an ultrastatic wormhole [i.e., $g_{00} \equiv 1 \Rightarrow \phi(r) = 0$ in equation (2.1)] with the "exotic" matter-energy confined to a thin layer, and we dispensed with the assumption of spherical symmetry.

We can now build a wormhole-stargate and affect *vm-Teleportation* such that a traveler stepping into the throat encounters **no** exotic matter-energy there. This will require that our wormhole be flat shaped. To make the wormhole flat requires that we choose the throat $\partial\Omega$ to have at least one flat face (picture the thin shell in Figure 3 becoming a flat shell). On that face the two principal radii of curvature become $\rho_1 = \rho_2 = \infty$ as required by standard geometry. Substituting this into equations (2.10a-c) gives

$$\sigma = \vartheta_1 = \vartheta_2 = 0 \qquad (2.11),$$

TELEPORTATION

which is a remarkable result. A further consequence of this is that now $K^i_j = 0$, thus making the Riemann curvature and stress-energy tensors (Riemann: $R^\alpha_\beta \sim K^\alpha_\beta$; stress-energy: $T^\alpha_\beta \sim K^\alpha_\beta$) at the throat become zero such that the associated δ-function singularities disappear there. This means that a traveler encountering and going through such a wormhole will feel no tidal gravitational forces and see no exotic matter-energy (that threads the throat). A traveler stepping through the throat will simply be _teleported_ into the other remote spacetime region or another universe (note: the Einstein equation does not fix the spacetime topology, so it is possible that wormholes are inter-universe as well as intra-universe tunnels). We construct such a _teleportation_ stargate by generating a thin shell or surface layer of "exotic" matter-energy much like a thin film of soap stretched across a loop of wire.

2.1.2 "Exotic" Matter-Energy Requirements

Now we have to estimate the amount of negative (or exotic) mass-energy that will be needed to generate and hold open a _vm-Teleportation_ wormhole. A simple formula originally due to Visser (1995) for short-throat wormholes using the thin shell formalism gives:

$$M_{wh} = -\frac{r_{throat}c^2}{G}$$

$$= -(1.3469 \times 10^{27}\, kg)\frac{r_{throat}}{1\, meter} \qquad (2.12),$$

$$= -(0.709\, M_{Jupiter})\frac{r_{throat}}{1\, meter}$$

where M_{wh} is the mass required to build the wormhole, r_{throat} is a suitable measure of the linear dimension (radius) of the throat, and $M_{Jupiter}$ is the mass of the planet Jupiter (1.90×10^{27} kg). Equation (2.12) demonstrates that a mass of $-0.709\, M_{Jupiter}$ (or -1.3469×10^{27} kg) will be required to build a wormhole 1 meter in size. As the wormhole size increases the mass requirement grows negative-large, and vice versa as the wormhole size decreases. After being alarmed by the magnitude of this, one should note that M_{wh} is **not** the total mass of the wormhole as seen by observers at remote distances. The non-linearity of the Einstein field equations dictates that the total mass is zero (actually, the total net mass being positive, negative or zero in the Newtonian approximation depending on the details of the negative energy configuration constituting the wormhole system). And finally, Visser et al. (2003) have demonstrated the existence of spacetime geometries containing traversable wormholes that are supported by **_arbitrarily small quantities_** of exotic matter-energy, and they proved that this was a general result. In Section 2.3 we will discuss how or whether we can create such a wormhole in the laboratory.

2.2 Engineering the Vacuum

Engineering the spacetime vacuum provides a second solution that also satisfies the definition of vm-Teleportation. The concept of "_engineering the vacuum_" was first introduced to the physics community by Lee (1988). Lee stated:

"_The experimental method to alter the properties of the vacuum may be called vacuum engineering...If indeed we are able to alter the vacuum, then we may encounter some new phenomena, totally unexpected._"

This new concept is based on the now-accepted fact that the vacuum is characterized by physical parameters and structure that constitutes an energetic medium which pervades the entire extent of the

TELEPORTATION

universe. We note here the two most important defining properties of the vacuum in this regard (Puthoff et al., 2002):

❑ Within the context of quantum field theory the vacuum is the seat of all energetic particle and field fluctuations.

❑ Within the context of general relativity theory the vacuum is the seat of a spacetime structure (or metric) that encodes the distribution of matter and energy.

We begin our look into this concept by examining the propagation of light through space. We know from quantum field theory that light propagating through space interacts with the vacuum quantum fields (a.k.a. vacuum quantum field fluctuations). The observable properties of light, including the speed of light, are determined by these interactions. Vacuum quantum interactions with light lead to an effect on the speed of light that is due to the absorption of photons (by the vacuum) to form virtual electron-positron pairs followed by the quick re-emission (from the vacuum) of the photon (see Figure 4). The virtual particle pairs are very short lived because of the large mismatch between the energy of a photon and the rest mass-energy of the particle pair. A key point is that this process makes a contribution to the observed vacuum permittivity ε_0 (and permeability μ_0) constant and, therefore, to the speed of light c [$c = (\varepsilon_0\mu_0)^{-1/2}$].

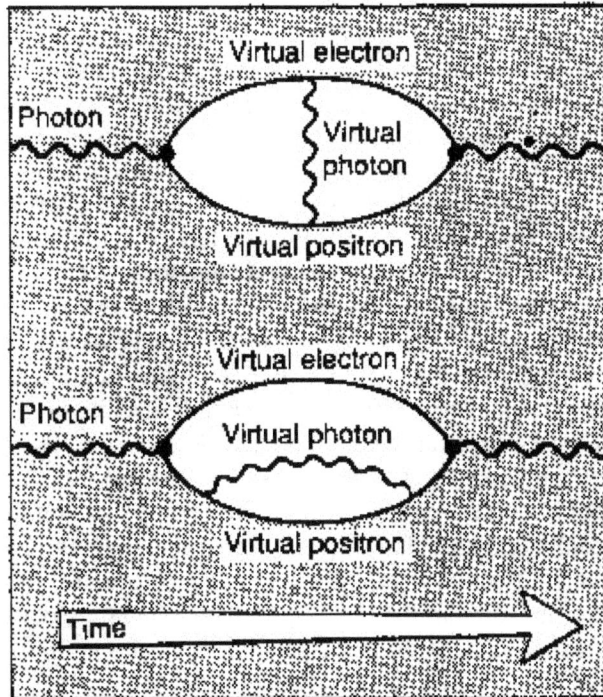

Photons can change into a variety of short-
lived, or "virtual", particles as they fly
through the vacuum. The processes above,
represented by Feynman diagrams, are "two-
loop" processes. They affect light's speed

Figure 4. A Schematic of Vacuum Quantum Field Fluctuations (a.k.a. Vacuum Zero Point Field Fluctuations) Involved in the "Light-by-Light" Scattering Process That Affects the Speed of Light (from Chown, 1990)

TELEPORTATION

The role of virtual particle pairs in determining the ε_0 (μ_0) of the vacuum is analogous to that of atoms/molecules in determining the relative permittivity ε (and μ) of a dielectric material. We know that the absorption/re-emission of photons by atoms/molecules in a transparent medium (note: there are no strongly absorbing resonances, so the atoms/molecules remain in their excited states for a very short time before re-emitting photons) is responsible for the refractive index of the medium, which results in the reduction of the speed of light for photons propagating through the medium. This absorption/re-emission process is also known in physics as a scattering process. We know from experiment that a change in the medium leads to a change in ε (μ), thus resulting in a change of the refractive index. The key point arising from this analogy is that a modification of the vacuum produces a change in ε_0 (μ_0) resulting in a subsequent change in c, and hence, a corresponding change in the vacuum refraction index.

Scharnhorst (1990) and Latorre et al. (1995) have since proved that the suppression of light scattering by virtual particle pairs (a.k.a. coherent light-by-light scattering) in the vacuum causes an ***increase*** in the speed of light accompanied by a decrease in the vacuum refraction index. This very unique effect is accomplished in a Casimir Effect capacitor cavity (or waveguide) whereby the vacuum quantum field fluctuations (a.k.a. zero-point fluctuations or ZPF) inside have been modified (becoming anisotropic and non-translational invariant) to satisfy the electromagnetic boundary conditions imposed by the presence of the capacitor plates (or waveguide walls). The principal result of this modification is the removal of the electromagnetic zero-point energy (ZPE) due to the suppression of vacuum ZPE modes with wavelengths longer than the cavity/waveguide cutoff ($\lambda_0 = 2d$, where d = plate separation; see Figure 5). This removal of free space vacuum ZPE modes suppresses the scattering of light by virtual particle pairs, thus producing the speed of light increase (and corresponding decrease in the vacuum refraction index). We know from standard optical physics and quantum electrodynamics (QED) that the optical phase and group velocities can exceed c under certain physical conditions, but dispersion always ensures that the signal velocity is $\leq c$. But recent QED calculations (see, Scharnhorst, 1990 and Latorre et al., 1995) have proved that in the Casimir Effect system, the dispersive effects are _much weaker_ still than those associated with the increase in c so that the phase, group and signal velocities will therefore _all increase_ by the same amount. Note that, in general, no dispersion shows up in all of the modified vacuum effects examined by investigators.

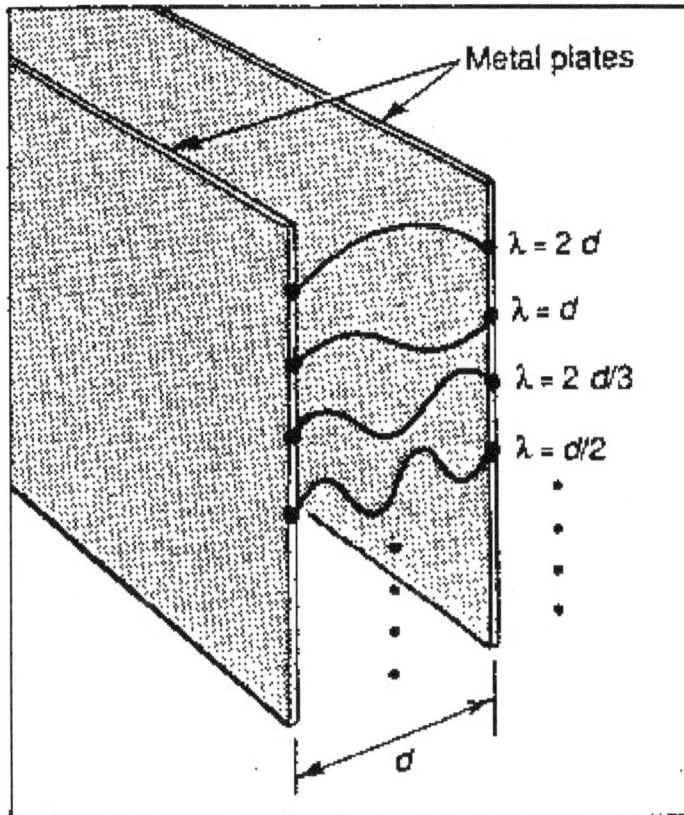

Casimir effect: the vacuum is full of virtual photons, but photons with wavelengths (λ), more than twice the separation of the plates, are excluded from the space between them. The imbalance pushes the plates together

Figure 5. A Schematic of the Casimir Effect Cavity/Waveguide (from Chown, 1990)

TELEPORTATION

Examples demonstrating the increase in light speed (decrease in vacuum refraction index) via the Casimir Effect vacuum and other modified vacuum effects, as well as those effects producing a decrease in light speed (increase in vacuum refraction index), are described as follows. The vacuum modification effect on the speed of light described in the previous paragraph is (Scharnhorst, 1990):

$$
\begin{aligned}
\frac{c_\perp^*}{c_0} &= \left(1 + \frac{11}{2^6 \bullet (45)^2} \frac{e^4}{(m_e a)^4}\right) \qquad (\hbar = c_0 = \varepsilon_0 = \mu_0 = 1) \\
&= \left(1 + \frac{11\pi^2}{8100} \alpha^2 \frac{1}{(m_e a)^4}\right) > 1
\end{aligned} \qquad (2.13),
$$

where $c_\perp^*$ is the (modified) speed of light propagation perpendicular to the Casimir Effect capacitor plates, c_0 is the speed of light in free space (3×10^8 m/s in MKS units), m_e is the electron mass, α is the fine structure constant ($\approx 1/137$), e is the electron charge ($e^2 = 4\pi\alpha$ in quantum field theory natural units), a is the plate separation, $\hbar$ is Planck's reduced constant, and ε_0 is the vacuum permittivity constant. The condition $\hbar = c_0 = \varepsilon_0 = \mu_0 = 1$ stresses that (2.13), and all the equations that follow, are in quantum field theory natural units. The speed of light and vacuum refraction index measured parallel to the plates is unchanged from their free space values ($c_\parallel = c_0$, $n_\parallel = n_0 = 1$). The modified vacuum refraction index measured perpendicular to the plates is (Scharnhorst, 1990):

$$
n_\perp = \left(1 - \frac{11}{2^6 \bullet (45)^2} \frac{e^4}{(m_e a)^4}\right) < 1 \qquad (\hbar = c_0 = \varepsilon_0 = \mu_0 = 1) \qquad (2.14).
$$

Equations (2.13) and (2.14) show that in general $n_\perp < 1$ and $c_\perp^* > c_0$. But $c_\perp^* \to c_0$ and $n_\perp \to 1$ when $a \to \infty$ as expected, since we are now allowing all of the vacuum ZPE modes to re-enter the Casimir cavity in this case.

We now survey the additional examples of modified vacuums which increase/decrease light speed (from Latorre et al., 1995):

- ❑ For light (photons) propagating in a Friedmann-Robertson-Walker (FRW) vacuum (i.e., a homogeneous and isotropic Robertson-Walker gravitational background with Friedmann cosmology):

$$
\frac{c^*}{c_0} = \left(1 + \frac{11}{45} \alpha G \frac{\rho_r + p}{m_e^2}\right) > 1 \qquad (\hbar = c_0 = \varepsilon_0 = \mu_0 = 1) \qquad (2.15),
$$

where c^* is the modified vacuum speed of light, G is Newton's constant, ρ_r is the energy density and p is the pressure of a radiation-dominated universe ($p = \rho_r/3$). Here the speed of light is increased.

- ❑ For light (photons) propagating in a homogeneous and isotropic thermal vacuum:

$$
\frac{c^*}{c_0} = \left(1 - \frac{44\pi^2}{2025} \alpha^2 \frac{T^4}{m_e^4}\right) < 1 \qquad (\hbar = c_0 = \varepsilon_0 = \mu_0 = k_B = 1) \qquad (2.16),
$$

where T is the temperature of the vacuum and k_B is the Boltzmann constant. Here the speed of light is decreased.

❑ For light (photons) propagating in an anisotropic vacuum given by an external constant uniform magnetic field $\boldsymbol{B}$:

$$\frac{c_{\parallel}^*}{c_0} = \left(1 - \frac{8}{45}\alpha^2 \frac{\boldsymbol{B}^2}{m_e^4}\sin^2\theta\right) < 1 \qquad (\hbar = c_0 = \varepsilon_0 = \mu_0 = 1)$$

$$\frac{c_{\perp}^*}{c_0} = \left(1 - \frac{14}{45}\alpha^2 \frac{\boldsymbol{B}^2}{m_e^4}\sin^2\theta\right) < 1$$

(2.17),

where the speed of light is decreased in this vacuum for polarizations coplanar ($\parallel$) with and perpendicular ($\perp$) to the plane defined by $\boldsymbol{B}$ and the direction of propagation, and θ is the angle between $\boldsymbol{B}$ and the direction of propagation. Latorre et al. (1995) calculated the polarization-average of (2.17) to give the averaged (modified) speed of light in the B-field:

$$\frac{c^*}{c_0} = \left(1 - \frac{22}{135}\alpha^2 \frac{\boldsymbol{B}^2}{m_e^4}\right) < 1 \qquad (\hbar = c_0 = \varepsilon_0 = \mu_0 = 1) \quad (2.18).$$

❑ For light (photons) propagating in an anisotropic vacuum given by an external constant uniform electric field $\boldsymbol{E}$, the polarization-averaged modified speed of light is:

$$\frac{c^*}{c_0} = \left(1 - \frac{22}{135}\alpha^2 \frac{\boldsymbol{E}^2}{m_e^4}\right) < 1 \qquad (\hbar = c_0 = \varepsilon_0 = \mu_0 = 1) \qquad (2.19).$$

Here the speed of light is decreased.

Equations (2.16) – (2.19) are the result of vacuum modifications that populate the vacuum with virtual or real particles that induce coherent (light-by-light) scattering, which reduces the speed of massless particles. By examining the form of equations (2.13) and (2.15) – (2.19) Latorre et al. (1995) discovered that the low energy modification of the speed of light is proportional to the ratio of the modified vacuum energy density (as compared to the standard vacuum energy density, $\rho_{vac} = 0$) over m_e^4, with a universal numerical coefficient and the corresponding coupling constants. And a general rule became apparent from their analysis that is applicable to modified vacua for massive and massless quantum field theories, for low energy:

$c^* > c_0$ (vacuum refraction index < 1) when the modified vacuum has a lower energy density
$c^* < c_0$ (vacuum refraction index > 1) when the modified vacuum has a higher energy density
$c^* = c_0$ (vacuum refraction index = 1) when the vacuum is free (or un-modified) with $\rho_{vac} = 0$

The first two rules explain the sign of the change of the speed of light. From this rule and the mathematical commonality between the form of (2.13) and (2.15) – (2.19) Latorre et al. (1995) found a single unifying expression to replace these equations:

$$\frac{c^*}{c_0} = 1 - \frac{44}{135}\alpha^2 \frac{\rho}{m_e^4} \qquad (\hbar = c_0 = \varepsilon_0 = \mu_0 = 1) \qquad (2.20),$$

TELEPORTATION

where ρ is the energy density of the modified vacua under consideration such that $\rho \rightarrow \rho_E \sim \mathbf{E}^2$ for the electric field vacuum, $\rho \rightarrow \rho_B \sim \mathbf{B}^2$ for the magnetic field vacuum, and $\rho \rightarrow \rho_T \sim \pi^2 T^4$ for the thermal vacuum. If the vacuum is a FRW gravitational vacuum, then one has to substitute one factor of α in (2.20) by $-m_e^2 G$ and $\rho \rightarrow \rho_r$. Equation (2.13) for the Casimir Effect vacuum studied earlier is recovered when $\rho \rightarrow \rho_{\text{Casimir}} = -(\pi^2/240)a^{-4}$.

Let us recast (2.20) into a more useful form. We subtract one from both sides of (2.20), do some algebra, and thus define the ratio of the change in the speed of light Δc in a modified vacuum to the speed of light in free space c_0:

$$\frac{c^*}{c_0} - 1 = \frac{c^* - c_0}{c_0} \equiv \frac{\Delta c}{c_0}$$

$$\frac{\Delta c}{c_0} = -\frac{44}{135}\alpha^2 \frac{\rho}{m_e^4} \qquad (\hbar = c_0 = \varepsilon_0 = \mu_0 = 1) \quad (2.21).$$

Equations (2.20) and (2.21) are in quantum field theory natural units, which is completely undesirable for estimating physically measurable values of $\Delta c/c_0$. We thus transform or "unwrap" (2.20) and (2.21) back into MKS or CGS units by making the following substitutions (Puthoff, 2003)

$$\rho \text{ (natural units)} \rightarrow \frac{\rho}{\hbar c} \text{ (MKS or CGS units)}$$

$$m_e \text{ (natural units)} \rightarrow \frac{m_e c}{\hbar} \text{ (MKS or CGS units)},$$

and after some algebra and rearranging we arrive at the final result:

$$\frac{c^*}{c_0} = 1 - \frac{44}{135}\alpha^2 \frac{\rho}{m_e c_0^2}\left(\frac{\hbar}{m_e c_0}\right)^3 \qquad (2.22)$$

and

$$\frac{\Delta c}{c_0} = -\frac{44}{135}\alpha^2 \frac{\rho}{m_e c_0^2}\left(\frac{\hbar}{m_e c_0}\right)^3 \qquad (2.23),$$

where all quantities are now in MKS or CGS units. We chose the former units so that $c_0 = 3\times10^8$ m/s, $\hbar = 1.055\times10^{-34}$ J-s, $m_e = 9.11\times10^{-31}$ kg, and $\alpha = 1/137$. Note that the ratio of the modified vacuum energy density to the electron rest-mass energy has the dimension of $(volume)^{-1}$ while the quantity in the bracket is the cubed Compton wavelength of the electron having the dimension of $(volume)$, and the product of these is dimensionless.

An excellent example for estimating the magnitude of the change in the speed of light (in a modified vacuum) is the Casimir Effect vacuum, since Casimir Effect experiments are common and widespread such that this would be ideal to experimentally test (2.23). We substitute the Casimir vacuum energy density $\rho_{\text{Casimir}} = -(\pi^2\hbar c_0/240)a^{-4}$ (in MKS units) into (2.23), do the algebra, insert the MKS values for the physical constants, and make further simplifications to get:

TELEPORTATION

$$\frac{\Delta c}{c_0} = -\frac{44}{135}\alpha^2\left(-\frac{\pi^2}{240}\frac{\hbar c_0}{a^4}\right)\frac{1}{m_e c_0^2}\left(\frac{\hbar}{m_e c_0}\right)^3$$

$$= \frac{11}{8100}\alpha^2\pi^2\left(\frac{\hbar}{m_e c_0 a}\right)^4 \qquad (2.24),$$

$$\approx \left(1.59\times10^{-56}\right)a^{-4}$$

where a (the plate separation) is in meters. Another useful equation is:

$$c^* = \left(1+\frac{\Delta c}{c_0}\right)c_0 \qquad (2.25),$$

where we make the substitution $c^* \to c_\perp^*$ for the present case. H. E. Puthoff and the author (Puthoff, 2003) compared the third line in (2.24) with equation (26) in Scharnhorst (1990) and discovered that the result cited there is in error, because the numerical coefficient is four orders of magnitude too small (Scharnhorst originally pointed out this error to Forward, 1996).

We now set $a = 10^{-6}$ m (1 μm) and we get $\Delta c/c_0 \approx 10^{-32}$ and $c_\perp^* \approx c_0$, which is a horrifically small 1 part in 10^{32} change that we cannot hope to measure at present. But for $a = 10^{-10}$ m (1 Å) we get $\Delta c/c_0 \approx 10^{-16}$ and $c_\perp^* \approx c_0$, which is a 1 part in 10^{16} change that could be measurable at present or in the very near future using high precision laser technology. Last, for $a = 1.1229\times10^{-14}$ m (11.229 fm or ≈ 11 times the nuclear diameter; 1 fm = 10^{-15} m) we find that $\Delta c/c_0 \approx 1$ and $c_\perp^* \approx 2c_0$. We are not able to do technical work at nuclear distances at this time; however, that could change as ultrahigh precision measurement technology continues to evolve. The threshold for the onset of significant changes in light speed occurs when $a < 10^{-12}$ m. This result is generally true for the other modified vacua surveyed in (2.15) – (2.19), since accessible (everyday) values for electric and magnetic field strengths, thermal temperatures and radiation densities are not large enough to overcome the size of the electron mass to create a measurable effect. However, there is a class of ultrahigh intensity tabletop lasers that have achieved such extreme electric and magnetic field strengths and temperatures that it may now be possible to consider using them to explore vacuum modification effects in the lab. We will return to this theme in a later section.

•**Key Point**: As disappointing as the Casimir Effect vacuum (and other modified vacua) results are, it should be strongly pointed out that special relativity theory says that if in one inertial reference frame an object travels only one part in 10^{16} (or even one part in 10^{32}) times faster than c_0, then one can find another reference frame where departure and arrival times of the object are simultaneous, and thus the velocity is ___*infinite*___. This is what motivates us to look at a teleportation mechanism based on engineering of the vacuum.

•**Technical Notes**.

> ➤ Equation (2.15) is interpreted as an increase in the speed of light due to a decrease in the number of vacuum ZPE modes. However, this effect is totally unrelated to light-by-light scattering in the vacuum because the gravitational background "squeezes" (as in squeezed quantum optics states; see Davis, 1999a) the ZPE modes, therefore reducing the vacuum energy density. We further note that the coefficient of 11 is the same for the gravitational vacuum as for the other modified vacua examples based on QED. This factor also appears in the coefficient of the Euler-Poincare characteristic spin-½ contribution to the gravitational trace anomaly (Birrell and Davies, 1982). It is beyond the scope of this study to consider the deep connections between quantum field theory and gravitation.

TELEPORTATION

➤ We have excluded from our survey the Latorre et al. (1995) results pertaining to all other (high or low energy) modifications of the speed of massless particles. That is because the other examples invoked different QED theories possessing massless ($m_e = 0$), massive and intrinsic mass scales that introduced complex correction terms (beyond the leading low energy terms surveyed above) which are mass-related or running mass-related, and they introduced no new speed modification effects (beyond the low energy electron-positron virtual pair contributions); or no genuine speed modification was possible (especially for the massless Quantum Chromodynamic sector involving pseudo-Goldstone particles).

➤ There is ongoing (very noisy) controversy within the physics community over the effects of $c^* > c_0$ on causality. As this topic is beyond the scope of this study, I will make three points in this regard: 1) There are no grounds for microcausality violations in accordance with Drummond and Hathrell (1980). 2) A new definition of causality is in order for FTL (faster-than-light) phenomena. 3) Investigators have found that time machines (a.k.a. closed timelike curves) do not affect Gauss's theorem, and thus do not affect the derivation of global conservation laws from differential ones (Friedman et al., 1990). The standard conservation laws remain globally valid while retaining a natural quasi-local interpretation for spacetimes possessing time machines (for example, asymptotically flat wormhole spacetimes). Thorne (1993) states that it may turn out that causality is violated at the macroscopic scale. Even if causality is obeyed macroscopically, then quantum gravity might offer finite probability amplitudes for microscopic spacetime histories possessing time machines. Li and Gott (1998) found a self-consistent vacuum for quantum fields in Misner space (a simple flat space with closed timelike curves), for which the renormalized stress-energy tensor is regular (in fact zero) everywhere. This implies that closed timelike curves could exist at least at the level of semi-classical quantum gravity theory. Therefore, FTL causality paradoxes are just a reflection of our ignorance or inadequate comprehension of the physics of chronology and causality.

In this section we have shown how "vacuum engineering" can modify the speed of light, and how this can, in principle, lead to vm-Teleportation. The vacuum modification concepts summarized above lead us to a formal theory that implements the concept of vacuum engineering within a framework that parallels general relativity theory. This theory is called the Polarizable-Vacuum Representation of General Relativity. In the next section we will introduce and summarize this theory.

2.2.1 The Polarizable-Vacuum Representation of General Relativity

The polarizable-vacuum representation of general relativity (a.k.a. PV-GR) treats the vacuum as a polarizable medium of variable refractive index (Puthoff, 1999a, 2002a, b; Puthoff et al., 2002) exemplifying the concept of the vacuum modification (or vacuum engineering) effects surveyed and discussed in the previous section. The PV-GR approach treats spacetime metric changes in terms of equivalent changes in the vacuum permittivity and permeability constants (ε_0 and μ_0), essentially along the lines of the "$TH\varepsilon\mu$" methodology (see Appendix B for a brief description of this) used in comparative studies of alternative metric theories of gravity (Lightman and Lee, 1973; Will, 1974, 1989, 1993; Haugan and Will, 1977). Such an approach, relying as it does on parameters familiar to engineers, can be considered a "metric engineering" approach. Maxwell's equations in curved space are treated in the isomorphism of a polarizable medium of variable refractive index in flat space (Volkov et al., 1971); the bending of a light ray near a massive body is modeled as due to an induced spatial variation in the refractive index of the vacuum near the body; the reduction in the velocity of light in a gravitational potential is represented by an effective increase in the refractive index of the vacuum, and so forth. This optical-engineering approach has been shown to be quite general (de Felice, 1971; Evans et al., 1996a, b).

TELEPORTATION

As recently elaborated by Puthoff (1999a, 2002a, b; Puthoff et al., 2002) the PV-GR approach, which was first introduced by Wilson (1921) and then developed by Dicke (1957, 1961), can be carried out in a self-consistent way so as to reproduce to appropriate order both the equations of general relativity and the match to the standard astrophysics weak-field experimental (PPN parameters and other) tests of those equations while posing testable modifications for strong-field conditions. It is in application that the PV-GR approach demonstrates its intuitive appeal and provides additional insight into what is meant by a curved spacetime metric.

Specifically, the PV-GR approach treats such measures as the speed of light, the length of rulers (atomic bond lengths), the frequency of clocks, particle masses, and so forth, in terms of a variable vacuum dielectric constant K in which the vacuum permittivity ε_0 transforms as $\varepsilon_0 \rightarrow K\varepsilon_0$ and the vacuum permeability transforms as $\mu_0 \rightarrow K\mu_0$ (see also, Rucker, 1977). In a planetary or solar gravitational potential $K = exp(2GM/rc_0^2) > 1$ (M is a local mass distribution, r is the radial distance from the center of M) while $K = 1$ in "empty" or free asymptotic space (Puthoff, 1999a, 2002a, b; Puthoff et al., 2002). In the former case, the speed of light is reduced, light emitted from an atom is redshifted as compared with a remote static atom (where $K = 1$), clocks run slower, objects/rulers shrink, etc. See Table 1.

Table 1. Metric Effects in the PV-GR Model When $K > 1$ (Compared With Reference Frames at Asymptotic Infinity Where $K = 1$; adapted from Puthoff et al., 2002)

Variable	Determining Equation (subscript 0 is asymptotic value where $K = 1$)	$K > 1$ (typical mass distribution, M)
modified speed of light $c^*(K)$	$c^* = c_0/K$	speed of light $< c_0$
Modified mass $m(K)$	$m = m_0 K^{3/2}$	effective mass increases
modified frequency $\omega(K)$	$\omega = \omega_0 K^{-1/2}$	redshift toward lower frequencies
modified time interval $\Delta t(K)$	$\Delta t = \Delta t_0 K^{1/2}$	clocks run slower
modified energy $E(K)$	$E = E_0 K^{-1/2}$	lower energy states
Modified length $L(K)$	$L = L_0 K^{-1/2}$	objects/rulers shrink
dielectric-vacuum "gravitational" forces $F(K)$	$F(K) \propto \nabla K$	attractive gravitational force

When $K = 1$ we have the condition that $c^* = c_0$ (vacuum refraction index = 1), because the vacuum is free (or un-modified, and $\rho_{vac} = 0$) in this case. When $K > 1$, as occurs in a region of space possessing a gravitational potential, then we have the condition that $c^* < c_0$ (vacuum refraction index > 1), because the modified vacuum has a higher energy density in the presence of the local mass distribution that generates the local gravitational field. This fact allows us to make a direct correspondence between the speed of light modification physics discussion in Section 2.2 and the underlying basis for the physics of the PV-GR model. Under certain conditions the spacetime metric can in principle be modified to reduce the value of K to below unity, thus allowing for faster-than-light (FTL) motion to be physically realized. In this case, the local speed of light (as measured by remote static observers) is increased, light emitted from an atom is blueshifted as compared with a remote static atom, objects/rulers expand, clocks run faster, etc. See Table 2. We therefore have the condition that $c^* > c_0$ (vacuum refraction index < 1) because the modified vacuum has a lower energy density. In fact, Puthoff (1999a, 2002a) has analyzed certain special black hole metrics and found $K < 1$ from the model. We will return to this theme later. In what follows we briefly review and summarize the key points and equations from the development of the PV-GR model, and we refer the reader to Puthoff (1999a, 2002a, b) for more extensive discussion and derivations.

Table 2. Metric Effects in the PV-GR Model When $K < 1$ (Compared With Reference Frames at Asymptotic Infinity Where $K = 1$; adapted from Puthoff et al., 2002)

Variable	**Determining Equation** (subscript 0 is asymptotic value where $K = 1$)	$K < 1$ *(typical mass distribution, M)*
modified speed of light $c^*(K)$	$c^* = c_0/K$	speed of light $> c_0$
modified mass $m(K)$	$m = m_0 K^{3/2}$	effective mass decreases
modified frequency $\omega(K)$	$\omega = \omega_0 K^{-1/2}$	blueshift toward higher frequencies
modified time interval $\Delta t(K)$	$\Delta t = \Delta t_0 K^{1/2}$	clocks run faster
modified energy $E(K)$	$E = E_0 K^{-1/2}$	higher energy states
modified length $L(K)$	$L = L_0 K^{-1/2}$	objects/rulers expand
dielectric-vacuum "gravitational" forces $F(K)$	$F(K) \propto \nabla K$	repulsive gravitational force

We begin by recalling that in flat space electrodynamics, the electric flux vector D in a linear, homogeneous medium can be written

$$\mathbf{D} = \varepsilon \mathbf{E}$$
$$= \varepsilon_0 \mathbf{E} + \mathbf{P} \qquad (2.26),$$
$$= \varepsilon_0 \mathbf{E} + \alpha_V \mathbf{E}$$

where ε is the permittivity of the medium, the polarization P corresponds to the induced dipole moment per unit volume in the medium whose polarizability per unit volume is α_V, and E is the electric field. The identical form of the last two terms naturally leads to the interpretation of ε_0 as the polarizability per unit volume of the vacuum. The quantum picture of the vacuum, where it has been shown that the vacuum acts as a polarizable medium by virtue of induced dipole moments resulting from the excitation of virtual electron-positron particle pairs (Heitler, 1954), completely justifies the interpretation that the vacuum is a medium. Note that there are other virtual particle pairs in the vacuum that also contribute to this picture; however, it is the electron-positron pairs that dominate the others, as shown in Section 2.2. The basic postulate of the PV-GR model for curved space conditions is that the polarizability of the vacuum in the vicinity of localized mass-energy distributions differs from its asymptotic free space value by virtue of vacuum polarization effects induced by the presence of the local mass-energy. Thus the postulate for the vacuum itself is

$$\mathbf{D} = \varepsilon \mathbf{E}$$
$$\equiv K \varepsilon_0 \mathbf{E} \qquad (2.27),$$

TELEPORTATION

where K (a function of position) is the modified dielectric constant of the vacuum due to the induced vacuum polarizability changes under consideration. Equation (2.27) defines the transformation $\varepsilon = K\varepsilon_0$.

Table 1 shows the various quantitative effects a polarizable vacuum (in the presence of positive mass-energy distributions) has on the various measurement processes important to general relativity. The effects demonstrated in the middle and right columns demonstrate the basis of the polarizable vacuum approach to general relativity. Table 2 shows what effects are manifested when negative mass-energy distributions induce vacuum polarizability changes that lead to FTL phenomenon. Experimental observations impose constraints on the model causing key physical constants to remain constant even with variable polarizability present in the local space. Puthoff (1999a, 2002a, b) has shown that the fine structure constant is constrained by observational data to remain constant within a variable polarizable vacuum, and this constraint actually defines the transformation $\mu = K\mu_0$. The elementary particle charge e is also taken to be constant in a variable polarizable vacuum because of charge conservation. And $\hbar$ remains a constant by conservation of angular momentum for circularly polarized photons propagating through the (variable polarizability) vacuum. The remaining constant of nature is the speed of light, and although the tables showed how this was modified in variable polarizability vacuums, it is interesting to see how this modification comes about. In a modified (variable polarizability) vacuum the speed of light is defined, as it is in standard electrodynamics, in terms of the permittivity and permeability by:

$$
\begin{aligned}
c^* &\equiv (\varepsilon\mu)^{-1/2} \\
&= (K\varepsilon_0 \cdot K\mu_0)^{-1/2} \\
&= (K^2\varepsilon_0\mu_0)^{-1/2} \\
&= \frac{1}{K}(\varepsilon_0\mu_0)^{-1/2} \\
&= \frac{c_0}{K}
\end{aligned}
\qquad (2.28),
$$

where the permittivity/permeability transformations and the free space (un-modified vacuum) definition for c_0 were inserted. Note that (2.28) can be re-written as $c^*/c_0 = 1/K$, and this is to be compared with (2.22). Thus we see from (2.28), and by comparison with (2.22), that K plays the role of a variable refractive index under conditions in which the vacuum polarizability is assumed to change in response to general relativistic-type influences. One further note of interest is that the permittivity/permeability transformations also maintains constant the ratio

$$
\sqrt{\frac{\mu}{\varepsilon}} = \sqrt{\frac{\mu_0}{\varepsilon_0}},
$$

which is the impedance of free space. This constant ratio is required to keep electric-to-magnetic energy ratios constant during adiabatic movement of atoms from one position in space to another of differing vacuum polarizability (Dicke, 1957, 1961). And this constant ratio is also a necessary condition in the $TH\varepsilon\mu$ formalism for an electromagnetic test particle to fall in a gravitational field with a composition-independent acceleration (Lightman and Lee, 1973; Will, 1974, 1989, 1993; Haugan and Will, 1977).

Now we make the "crossover connection" to the standard spacetime metric tensor concept that characterizes conventional general relativity theory, as originally shown by Puthoff (1999a, 2002a, b). In flat (un-modified or free) space the standard four-dimensional infinitesimal spacetime interval ds^2 is given (in Cartesian coordinates with subscript 0) by

TELEPORTATION

$$ds^2 = -c_0^2 dt_0^2 + \sum_{i=1}^{3} dx_{i0}^2 \qquad (2.29),$$

where $i \equiv (1 = x, 2 = y, 3 = z)$. This metric means that measuring rods and clocks are non-varying wherever one goes in spacetime to make measurements. However, this has been shown to be incorrect in general relativity theory, so the length and time transformations (between proper and coordinate values) given in the tables (middle columns) indicate that measuring rods and clocks do vary when placed in regions where $K \neq 1$. Therefore, we replace the time and space differentials in (2.29) with the length and time transformations in the tables into (2.29), and derive the general relativistic spacetime interval

$$ds^2 = -\frac{1}{K} c_0^2 dt^2 + K \left(\sum_{i=1}^{3} dx_i^2 \right) \qquad (2.30).$$

Note that observers within a $K \neq 1$ region will always measure the speed of light to be c_0. Equation (2.30) defines an isotropic coordinate system, which is a common and useful way to represent spacetime metrics in general relativity studies. By inspection the metric tensor is written

$$g_{\alpha\beta} = \begin{pmatrix} -1/K & 0 & 0 & 0 \\ 0 & K & 0 & 0 \\ 0 & 0 & K & 0 \\ 0 & 0 & 0 & K \end{pmatrix} \qquad (2.31).$$

The Lagrangian density for matter-field interactions in a vacuum of variable K is given by Puthoff (1999a, 2002a, b) as

$$L_d = -\left[\frac{m_0 c_0^2}{\sqrt{K}} \sqrt{1 - \left(\frac{v}{c_0/K} \right)^2} + q\Phi - qA_i v^i \right] \delta^3(\mathbf{r} - \mathbf{r}_0)$$
$$-\frac{1}{2}\left(\frac{\mathbf{B}^2}{K\mu_0} - K\varepsilon_0 \mathbf{E}^2 \right) - \frac{c_0^4}{32\pi G} \frac{1}{K^2}\left[(\nabla K)^2 - \frac{1}{(c_0/K)^2}\left(\frac{\partial K}{\partial t} \right)^2 \right] \qquad (2.32),$$

where the first term is the Lagrangian density for a free particle of mass m_0, charge q and 3-vector velocity v ($v = |\mathbf{v}|$, 3-vector components are labeled by i) interacting with electromagnetic fields via the electromagnetic field 4-vector potential $A_\mu = (\Phi, A_i)$ (note that $\delta^3(\mathbf{r} - \mathbf{r}_0)$ is the delta function that locates the point particle at position $\mathbf{r} = \mathbf{r}_0$); the second term is the Lagrangian density for the electromagnetic fields themselves, and the last term is the Lagrangian density for K (treated here as a scalar variable). This last term emulates the Lagrangian density for the gravitational field. Equation (2.32) does not include any quantum gauge field interaction terms because it is beyond the scope of the present incarnation of the PV-GR approach to include them. We can obtain the equations of particle motion in a variable dielectric vacuum by performing the standard variations of the Lagrangian density $\delta(\int L_d \, dx \, dy \, dz \, dt)$ with respect to the particle variables. However, we are more interested in obtaining the "master equation" for K by varying the Lagrangian density with respect to K, and Puthoff (1999a, 2002a, b) gives the result:

TELEPORTATION

$$\nabla^2 \sqrt{K} - \frac{1}{(c_0/K)^2} \frac{\partial^2 \sqrt{K}}{\partial t^2}$$

$$= -\frac{8\pi G}{c_0^4} \sqrt{K} \left\{ \frac{\left(m_0 c_0^2 / \sqrt{K}\right)}{\sqrt{1 - \left(\frac{v}{c_0/K}\right)^2}} \frac{1}{2} \left[1 + \left(\frac{v}{c_0/K}\right)^2 \right] \delta^3(\mathbf{r} - \mathbf{r}_0) \right.$$

$$\left. + \frac{1}{2} \left(\frac{\mathbf{B}^2}{K\mu_0} + K\varepsilon_0 \mathbf{E}^2 \right) - \frac{c_0^4}{32\pi G} \frac{1}{K^2} \left[(\nabla K)^2 + \frac{1}{(c_0/K)^2} \left(\frac{\partial K}{\partial t} \right)^2 \right] \right\}$$

(2.33).

This equation describes the generation of general relativistic vacuum polarization effects due to the presence of matter and fields. By inspecting the right-hand side of the equation, we observe that changes in K are driven by the mass density (1st term), electromagnetic energy density (2nd term), and the vacuum polarization energy density itself (3rd term). In fact, the 3rd term emulates the gravitational field self-energy density. Note that the 2nd and 3rd terms in (2.33) appear with opposite signs with the result that electromagnetic field effects can counteract the gravitational field effects. Puthoff found that (2.33) gives the solution $K = exp(2GM/rc_0^2)$ in the vicinity of a static spherically symmetric (uncharged) mass M (in the low velocity limit $v \ll c_0$, $\partial K/\partial t = 0$, $E = B = 0$, $q = 0$), which reproduces to appropriate order the standard general relativistic Schwarzschild spacetime metric for the weak gravitational field conditions prevailing in the solar system. This solution guarantees that $K > 1$ near mass concentrations.

Of major importance to the present study are solutions giving $K < 1$ so that teleportation can be realized. Puthoff has found one such solution by studying the case of a static spherically symmetric mass M with charge Q familiar from the study of the Reissner-Nordstrøm spacetime metric. In this case Puthoff found the result

$$K = \left[\cos\left(\frac{\sqrt{b^2 - a^2}}{r}\right) + \frac{a}{\sqrt{b^2 - a^2}} \sin\left(\frac{\sqrt{b^2 - a^2}}{r}\right) \right]^2 \qquad (b^2 > a^2) \qquad (2.34),$$

where $a^2 = (GM/c_0^2)^2$, $b^2 = Q^2 G/4\pi\varepsilon_0 c_0^4$, and r is the radial distance from the center of M. And in this case (2.34) gives $K < 1$, which shows that FTL solutions are available in the PV-GR approach (as they are also in the Einstein theory). (For $a^2 > b^2$ the solution is hyperbolic-trigonometric and describes the standard Reissner-Nordstrøm metric where $K > 1$.)

Generally speaking, in Einstein general relativity the Reissner-Nordstrøm metric can be manipulated along with two shells of electrically charged matter to form a traversable wormhole (Schein and Aichelburg, 1996). But there are two drawbacks to this. The first is that the scheme involves dealing with the collapsed state of the stellar matter that generates the metric (a.k.a. Reissner-Nordstrøm black hole) along with the unpleasant side effects that are encountered, such as the crushing singularities and multiple (unstable) event horizons. Second, the traversable wormhole is an eternal time machine connecting remote regions of the same universe together. Now there are no black hole solutions found in the PV-GR model because in that approach stellar matter collapses smoothly to an ultra-dense state and without the creation of singularities and event horizons (Puthoff, 1999b).

In either case, the Reissner-Nordstrøm metric does not offer a viable mechanism for vm-Teleportation. We are more interested in examining other PV-GR cases (where $K < 1$ or even $K \ll 1$)

that emulate the effects of traversable wormhole metrics that do obey the vm-Teleportation definition, such as the example presented in Section 2.1. Equation (2.33) suggests that we search for a vacuum engineering concept that exploits electromagnetic fields to alter the vacuum dielectric constant K to induce the desired vm-Teleportation effect in the modified vacuum. (However, we can insert other source terms that will lead to the desired result.) We envision this particular teleportation concept to resemble Figure 2. [Note: Before this report went to press H. E. Puthoff, C. Maccone and the author discovered a number of $K < 1$ solutions to equation (2.33) that uniquely meet the definition of vm-Teleportation and FTL motion. We discovered that the generic energy density required to generate $K < 1$ solutions must be negative, and that the total energy density of the system as seen by remote observes is approximately zero. This unique result compares very well with the traversable wormhole mass-energy density requirements discussed in Section 2.1.2. This discovery will be the subject of a forthcoming paper.]

2.3 Conclusion and Recommendations

The concept we envision for vm-Teleportation is that animate or inanimate objects would be placed inside an environmentally enclosed vessel that would simply be moved into the teleportation device. The "teleporter" would be activated, and the vessel would almost immediately disappear and then reappear at the remote destination as if it were briefly moving through a portal or "stargate." The teleportation device might be required to operate in the vacuum of space outside of the Earth's atmosphere. We have shown two practically equivalent ways to implement vm-Teleportation. There is the manipulation of spacetime geometry via exploiting negative (i.e., quantum vacuum zero point) energy as shown by Einstein's general relativity theory, and there is the modification of the vacuum dielectric constant as shown by the PV-GR model. Both have a great deal of theoretical foundation to begin exploring experimentally. The PV-GR model needs additional theoretical work for the present application, but it is now mature enough for experimental exploration.

There already is extensive theoretical, and more importantly, experimental research proving that the vacuum can be engineered (or physically modified) so that the vacuum ZPE can be exploited (via the Casimir Effect, for example) to extract electrical energy or actuate microelectromechanical devices (see for example, Ambjørn and Wolfram, 1983; Forward, 1984, 1996, 1998; Puthoff, 1990, 1993; Cole and Puthoff, 1993; Milonni, 1994; Mead and Nachamkin, 1996; Lamoreaux, 1997; Chan et al., 2001, and the references cited therein). But most of this research involves very low energy density regimes, which are much too low for our purposes. The Mead and Nachamkin (1996) device is actually designed to extract electrical energy from the higher frequency/higher energy density ZPE modes. However, new ultrahigh-intensity lasers became available in the 1990s that have achieved extreme physical conditions in the lab that are comparable to the extreme astrophysical conditions expected to be found in stellar cores and on black hole event horizons (Perry, 1996; Mourou et al., 1998; Perry, 2000). The power intensity of these lasers has reached the point to where they actually probe QED vacuum physics and general relativistic physics, and they have even modified the vacuum itself. The lasers were originally called petaWatt lasers (operating range of $10^{14} - 10^{18}$ Watts/cm^2 at femtosecond pulses), but they have now reached power intensity levels in the $10^{25} - 10^{30}$ Watts/cm^2 range. The lasers were made possible by a novel breakthrough called "chirped pulse amplification" whereby the initial low energy/low power intensity laser beam is stretched, amplified and then compressed without experiencing any beam distortions or amplifier damage. This laser system was initially designed as a large-optics beam-line power booster for the NOVA laser fusion experiment at Lawrence Livermore National Laboratory. But researchers found a way to shrink the optics down to tabletop scale, and one can now own and operate a tabletop ultrahigh-intensity laser for $\approx$ \$500,000. The dimensions of the optical bench used by the University of California-San Diego is $\approx$ 5 m $\times$ 12 m (or $\approx$ 60 m^2; see Mourou et al., 1998). In tabletop lab experiments ultrahigh-intensity lasers have generated $\gg$ gigagauss magnetic fields, $\geq 10^{16}$ Volt/cm electric field strengths, $\gg$ terabar light pressures and $\gg 10^{22}$ m/sec^2 subatomic particle accelerations. These ultrahigh-intensity

TELEPORTATION

tabletop lasers are thus the ideal instrument with which to explore the fundamental physics underlying the two possible concepts for vm-Teleportation.

There are several ideas on how to generate negative energy in the lab that could potentially be extracted and concentrated in the proper fashion to induce the traversable flat-face wormhole outlined in Section 2.1.1 or induce the $K < 1$ condition (in the PV-GR model) outlined in Section 2.2.1. The schemes for generating negative energy are:

❑ Casimir Effect (described in Section 2.2): This is the easiest and most well known way to generate negative energy in the lab. The energy density $\rho_{\text{Casimir}} = -(\pi^2 \hbar c_0/240)a^{-4}$ within a Casimir capacitor cavity is negative and manifests itself by producing a force of attraction between the capacitor plates. This has been measured in the lab (see above references). Forward (1998) proposes a mechanism for the endless extraction of energy from the vacuum in a Casimir cavity by cyclic manipulation of the cavity dimensions.

❑ Moving Mirror: Negative quantum vacuum energy can be created by a single moving reflecting surface (a moving mirror). If a mirror moves with increasing acceleration, then a flux of negative energy emanates from its surface and flows out into the space ahead of the mirror (Birrell and Davies, 1982). However, this effect is known to be exceedingly small, and it is not the most effective way to generate negative energy.

❑ Optically Squeezed Laser Light: Negative quantum vacuum energy can also be generated by an array of ultrahigh intensity lasers with an ultrafast rotating mirror system. In this scheme a laser beam is passed through an optical cavity resonator made of lithium niobate crystal that is shaped like a cylinder with rounded silvered ends to reflect light. The resonator will act to produce a secondary lower frequency light beam in which the pattern of photons is rearranged into pairs. This is the quantum optical "squeezing" of light effect. (See Section A.2 in Appendix A for a complete definition and description of squeezed quantum states.) Therefore, the squeezed light beam emerging from the resonator will contain pulses of negative energy interspersed with pulses of positive energy. Another way to squeeze light would be to manufacture extremely reliable light pulses containing precisely one, two, three, etc. photons apiece and combine them together to create squeezed states to order. Superimposing many such states could theoretically produce bursts of intense negative energy. For the laser beam resonator example we find that both negative and positive energy pulses are of $\approx 10^{-15}$ second duration. We could arrange a set of rapidly rotating mirrors to separate the positive and negative energy pulses from each other. The light beam is to strike each mirror surface at a very shallow angle while the rotation ensures that the negative energy pulses are reflected at a slightly different angle from the positive energy pulses. A small spatial separation of the two different energy pulses will occur at some distance from the rotating mirror. Another system of mirrors will be needed to redirect the negative energy pulses to an isolated location and concentrate them there.

❑ Gravitationally Squeezed Vacuum Energy: A natural source of negative quantum vacuum energy comes from the effect that gravitational fields (of astronomical bodies) in space have upon the surrounding vacuum. For example, the gravitational field of the Earth produces a zone of negative energy around it by dragging some of the virtual particle pairs (a.k.a. virtual photons or vacuum ZPF) downward. This concept was initially developed in the 1970s as a byproduct of studies on quantum field theory in curved space (Birrell and Davies, 1982). However, Hochberg and Kephart (1991) derived an important application of this concept to the problem of creating and stabilizing traversable wormholes, and their work was corrected and extended by Davis (1999a). They proved that one can utilize the negative vacuum energy densities, which arise from *distortion of the electromagnetic zero point fluctuations* due to the interaction with a prescribed gravitational background, for providing a violation of the energy conditions (see

TELEPORTATION

Section A.1 in Appendix A). Hochberg and Kephart (1991) showed that the squeezed quantum states of quantum optics provide a natural form of matter having negative energy density. And since the vacuum is defined to have vanishing energy density, anything possessing less energy density than the vacuum must have a negative energy density. The analysis, via quantum optics, shows that gravitation itself provides the mechanism for generating the squeezed vacuum states needed to support stable traversable wormholes. The production of negative energy densities via a squeezed vacuum is a necessary and unavoidable consequence of the interaction or coupling between ordinary matter and gravity, and this defines what is meant by gravitationally squeezed vacuum states. The magnitude of the gravitational squeezing of the vacuum can be estimated from the squeezing condition, which simply states that substantial gravitational squeezing of the vacuum occurs for those quantum electromagnetic field modes with *wavelength* (λ in meters) > *Schwarzschild radius* (r_S in meters) of the mass in question (whose gravitational field is squeezing the vacuum). The Schwarzschild radius is the critical radius, according to general relativity theory, at which a spherically symmetric massive body becomes a black hole; i.e., at which light is unable to escape from the body's surface. We can actually choose any radial distance from the mass in question to perform this analysis, but using the Schwarzschild radius makes equations simpler in form. The general result of the gravitational squeezing effect is that as the gravitational field strength increases the negative energy zone (surrounding the mass) also increases in strength. Table 3 shows when gravitational squeezing becomes important for example masses. The table shows that in the case of the Earth, Jupiter and the Sun, this squeeze effect is extremely feeble because only ZPF mode wavelengths above 0.2 m – 78 km are affected. For a solar mass black hole (radius of 2.95 km), the effect is still feeble because only ZPF mode wavelengths above 78 km are affected. But note from the table that quantum black holes with Planck mass will have enormously strong negative energy surrounding them because all ZPF mode wavelengths above 8.50×10^{-34} meter will be squeezed; in other words, all wavelengths of interest for vacuum fluctuations. Black holes with proton mass will have the strongest negative energy zone in comparison because the squeezing effect includes all ZPF mode wavelengths above 6.50×10^{-53} meter. Furthermore, a black hole smaller than a nuclear diameter ($\approx 10^{-16}$ m) and containing the mass of a mountain ($\approx 10^{11}$ kg) would possess a fairly strong negative energy zone because all ZPF mode wavelengths above 10^{-15} meter will be squeezed.

Table 3. Substantial Gravitational Squeezing Occurs When
$\lambda \geq 8\pi r_S$ (For Electromagnetic ZPF; adapted from Davis, 1999a)

Mass of body	Schwarzschild radius of body, r_S	ZPF mode wavelength, λ
Sun = 2.0×10^{30} kg	2.95 km	≥ 78 km
Jupiter = 1.9×10^{27} kg	2.82 m	≥ 74 m
Earth = 5.976×10^{24} kg	8.87×10^{-3} m	≥ 0.23 m
Typical mountain $\approx 10^{11}$ kg	$\approx 10^{-16}$ m	$\geq 10^{-15}$ m
Planck mass = 2.18×10^{-8} kg	3.23×10^{-35} m	$\geq 8.50 \times 10^{-34}$ m
Proton = 1.673×10^{-27} kg	2.48×10^{-54} m	$\geq 6.50 \times 10^{-53}$ m

●**Recommendations**:

➢ <u>Theoretical Program 1</u>: A one to two year theoretical study (cost $\approx$ \$80,000) should be initiated to explore the recently discovered $K < 1$ (FTL) solutions to equation (2.33) in order to define, characterize and model the negative energy density source(s) that induce the FTL vacuum modification. The study should also identify potential lab experiments designed to test theoretical predictions.

➤ Theoretical Program 2: A one to two year study (cost ≈ $80,000) should be initiated to conduct a detailed review of the negative energy generation schemes summarized above to define their characteristics, performances and requirements. The study should develop technical parameters for each of the schemes in order to identify potential lab experiments.

➤ Experimental Program 1: An experimental study should be conducted to test Forward's (1998) Casimir energy extraction proposal. An experiment definition study will be required to estimate the experimental method, procedure, equipment needs and costs.

➤ Experimental Program 2: An experimental study using ultrahigh-intensity lasers should be conducted to test the Optically Squeezed Laser Light proposal. An experiment definition study will be required to estimate the experimental method, procedure, equipment needs and costs.

➤ Experimental Program 3: An experimental study using ultrahigh-intensity lasers should be conducted to probe QED vacuum physics and vacuum modification as well as test elements of the PV-GR model. A starting point for this program would be to use such lasers to perform the Ding and Kaplan (1989, 1992, 2000; see also, Forward, 1996) experiment. This is an important fundamental physics experiment to do, because it can distinguish between the rival quantum vacuum electromagnetic ZPE fluctuation and fluctuating charged particle source field theory models, which would settle the acrimonious debate over whether the vacuum really fluctuates or not. R. L. Forward (1999) told the author that a Nobel Prize rides on performing this experiment and settling the issue once and for all. The Ding and Kaplan proposal is already designed to probe QED vacuum physics and vacuum modification. [The essence of the Ding and Kaplan proposal is to demonstrate that a form of photon-photon scattering predicted by QED gives rise to 2nd-harmonic generation of intense laser radiation in a DC magnetic field due to the broken symmetry of interaction (in the Feynman "box" diagram approximation). This effect is possible only when the field system (optical wave + DC field) is inhomogeneous, in particular when a Gaussian laser beam propagates in either a homogeneous or inhomogeneous DC magnetic field. In other words, a vacuum region is filled with a DC magnetic field that polarizes the virtual particle pairs (a.k.a. virtual photons) in the vacuum. This polarized vacuum then scatters incident ultrahigh-intensity laser photons of frequency ν (energy E), thereby generating outgoing photons of frequency 2ν (energy $2E$).] An experiment definition study will be required to estimate the experimental method, procedure, equipment needs and costs.

➤ Experimental Program 4: An experimental study using ultrahigh-intensity lasers should be conducted to establish the extreme physical conditions necessary to test the strong-field limit of general relativity with an emphasis on generating spacetime curvature and negative energy in order to induce a putative micro-wormhole. (Experimental Programs 3 and 4 could be done together to determine whether Puthoff's PV-GR theory or Einstein's general relativity theory is the correct model for nature.) A Nobel Prize is in the offing if this question were to be addressed and settled. An experiment definition study will be required to estimate the experimental method, procedure, equipment needs and costs.

TELEPORTATION

3.0 q-TELEPORTATION

3.1 Teleportation Scenario

Future space explorers and their equipment will need to easily and quickly travel from an orbiting spacecraft to the surface of some remote planet in order to get their work done, or military personnel in the United States need to easily and quickly travel from their military base to another remote location on Earth in order to participate in a military operation, or space colonists will need quick transport to get from Earth to their new home planet. Instead of using conventional transportation to expedite travel the space explorer, military personnel or space colonist and/or their equipment go into the "Teleporter" (a.k.a. "Transporter" in Star Trek lingo) and are "beamed down" or "beamed over" to their destinations at light speed. The mechanism for this teleportation process is hypothetically envisioned to be the following:

1. Animate/inanimate objects placed inside the teleporter are scanned by a computer-generated and -controlled beam.

2. The scan beam encodes the entire quantum information contained within the animate/inanimate object(s) into organized bits of information, thus forming a digital pattern of the object(s).

3. The scan beam then dematerializes the object(s) and stores its pattern in a pattern buffer, thus transforming the atomic constituents of the dematerialized object(s) into a matter stream. Alternative 1: The dematerialization process converts the atoms into a beam of pure energy. Alternative 2: The scan beam does not dematerialize the object(s).

4. The teleporter then transmits the matter/pure energy stream and quantum information signal in the form of an annular confinement beam to its destination. Alternative: Only the quantum information signal is transmitted.

5. At the receiving teleporter the matter/pure energy stream is sent into a pattern buffer whereby it is recombined with its quantum information, and the object(s) is rematerialized back into its original form. Alternative 1: The receiving teleporter recombines the transmitted quantum information with atoms stored inside a reservoir to form a copy of the original. Alternative 2: The quantum information is reorganized in such a way as to display the object on some three-dimensional (holographic) visual display system.

Problem: This generic scenario is modeled after teleportation schemes found in SciFi. There are a lot of important little details that were left out of the teleportation process because we simply do not know what they are. This technology does not yet exist. And we are left with the question of which one of the alternative processes identified in items 3 – 5 one wants to choose from. The above scenario is only an outline, and it is by no means complete since it merely serves to show what speculation exists on the subject. The above scenario describes a speculative form of what we call *q-Teleportation*.

There are questions to be addressed in the above scenario. Does the teleporter transmit the atoms and the quantum bit information signal that comprises the animate/inanimate object or just the quantum bit information signal? There are $\approx 10^{28}$ atoms of matter combined together in a complex pattern to form a human being. How does one transmit this much information and how do we disassemble that many atoms? Computer information gurus would insist that it is not the atoms that matter but only the bits of

TELEPORTATION

information representing them when considering the transmission of large "bodies" of information. But are humans simply the sum of all the atoms (and the related excited atom quantum states) that comprise them? We could possibly learn to reconstitute a beam of atoms into a chemically accurate human being. However, would this also include the reconstruction of a person's consciousness (personality, memories, hopes, dreams, etc.) and soul or spirit? This question is beyond the scope of this study to address, but it is nevertheless one of the most important concepts awaiting a complete scientific understanding.

For the teleporter to process and transmit the quantum bit information signal that encodes the animate/inanimate object's pattern will require stupendous digital computer power. For each atom comprising the object we must encode its location in space (three position coordinates), its linear and angular momentum (three vector components for each quantity), and its internal quantum state (electron orbital-energy levels and their excitation/de-excitation and ionization states, binding to other atoms to form molecules, molecular vibrational/rotational states, bound nuclei states, spin states for electrons and nuclei, etc.), etc. If we assume that we can digitally encode all of this information for a single atom with a minimum of one kilobyte (1 byte = 8 bits, 1 bit $\equiv$ 0 or 1) of data, then we will require a minimum of 10^{28} kilobytes to encode and store an entire human being (in three-dimensions). To digitally store and access this much information at present (and for the foreseeable future) is nontrivial. It will take more than 2,400 times the present age of the universe ($\approx$ 13 billion years) to access this amount of data using commercially available computers (operating at $\approx$ 10 gigabyte/sec). Top-of-the-line supercomputers will not reduce this time significantly. The computer technology needed to handle such a large data storage requirement simply does not exist. The largest commercially available computers can store $\approx$ 40 gigabytes on a single hard drive. We will need $\approx 10^{20}$ of these hard drives to store the encoded information of just one human being. Also, wire and coaxial/fiber optic cables do not have the physical capacity to transmit this amount of data between devices. These numbers will not be significantly different for macroscopic inanimate objects. The information processing and transfer technology required for the teleportation system may become possible in 200 – 300 years if improvements in computer storage and speed maintains a factor of 10 – 100 increase for every decade. There is speculation that emergent molecular, bio-molecular (DNA-based systems) and quantum computer technology may achieve the performances required for a teleportation system. In the former case molecular dynamics mimics computer logic processes and the $\approx 10^{25}$ particles in a macroscopic sample will all act simultaneously, making for far greater digital information processing and transfer speeds. Researchers have given no formal performance estimates for this emergent technology. In the latter case quantum computing would take advantage of entangled quantum states of subatomic matter or photons, whereby digital logic processes would occur at light speed. This technology is in its infancy, and there has been no clear direction on what performance levels will be possible in the future. This topic will be discussed further in Section 3.2.3.

In the above teleportation scenario we might consider dematerializing animate/inanimate objects into a matter stream consisting of only the object's constituent atoms or atomic subcomponents (protons, neutrons and electrons) and transmitting them at the speed of light (or close to it). To push atoms or subatomic particles to near the speed of light will require imparting to them an energy comparable to their rest-mass energy, which will be at a minimum of one order of magnitude larger than the amount of energy required to break protons up into free quarks. The energy required to completely dematerialize (or dissolve) matter into its basic quantum constituents or into pure energy is alone stupendous. At first one will have to impart to every molecule within the object an energy that is equivalent to the binding energy between atoms (atomic binding energy ~ chemical energy ~ *several* eV) in order to break apart the molecules comprising the object's macro-structure. After this an energy equivalent to nuclear binding energies ($\approx$ *several* $\times 10^6$ times atomic binding energy, or $\approx$ *several* MeV) must be imparted to every free atomic nucleus inside the object in order to break apart the protons and neutrons residing within each nucleus. And last, an energy equivalent to the binding energy that holds together the three quarks residing within each proton and neutron must be imparted to each of the free protons and neutrons within the object. According to the Standard Model and experimental data, the quark binding energy is

TELEPORTATION

practically infinite. But all is not lost, because the Standard Model also predicts that if we could heat up the nuclei to $\approx 10^{13}$ °C ($\approx 10^6$ times hotter than the core temperature of the Sun, or $\approx 10^3$ MeV), then the quarks inside would suddenly lose their binding energies and become massless (along with other elementary matter). This heat is also equivalent to the rest-mass energy of protons and neutrons. Therefore, to heat up and dematerialize one human being would require the annihilation of the rest mass-energy of all 10^{28} protons-neutrons or the energy equivalent of 330 1-megaton thermonuclear bombs. Compare this stupendous explosive energy with the explosive yield of the largest thermonuclear bomb ever detonated on Earth, which was a 50-megaton bomb that was built by Andrei Sakharov in the USSR and detonated on October 30, 1961; it was called "Tzar Bomba." Its first incarnation (ca. early October 1961) comprised a uranium fusion tamper, which gave an estimated explosive yield of ≈ 100 megatons. But the weapon was too heavy (27 metric tons) for a bomber to carry, so the tamper was replaced by one made of lead, which reduced both the weight and the yield. In the end we see that it is not a trivial problem to simply heat up and dematerialize any human or inanimate objects. The technology to do so does not exist unless we invoke new physics to get around the energy requirement.

Finally, we must consider the resolution and aperture of the optics required to scan and transmit the animate/inanimate object's matter (or energy) stream. The Heisenberg quantum uncertainty principle fundamentally constrains the measurement resolution of conjugate observable quantities, such as position and momentum or energy and time. The measurement of any combination of (conjugate) observables with arbitrarily high precision is not possible, because a high precision measurement of one observable leads to imprecise knowledge of the value of the conjugate observable. The quantum uncertainty principle makes it impossible to measure the exact, total quantum state of any object with certainty. The scan resolution of a teleportation system is defined by the wavelength of light used to illuminate the object's atomic/subatomic constituents and record their configurations. To resolve matter at atomic/subatomic distance scales requires that the energy of the scanner light (photons) be extremely large (according to the uncertainty principle); and during the scan this large light energy will be conveyed to the constituents, causing them to drastically change their speed and direction of motion. This means that it is physically impossible to resolve an object's atomic/subatomic particle components and their configurations with the precision necessary to accurately encode and later recreate the object being teleported. To resolve atomic/subatomic particles requires wavelengths smaller than the size of these constituents, which will typically be 1 Å – 1 fm. Such wavelengths are in the gamma ray part of the spectrum, and this becomes a major technical problem for us because at present there is no gamma ray electro-optics with which to work with. Now consider the example of teleporting an object from the surface of a planet back to its spacecraft in orbit some *several* $\times 10^2 - 10^3$ km away. The optical aperture required to illuminate and scan an object with ≈ 1 Å – 1 fm resolution from orbit will be >> *several* $\times 10^2 - 10^3$ km. If we are to consider teleporting an object from planet to planet or from star to star then the aperture required will be >> *several* $\times 10^8 - 10^{13}$ km. These technical problems are truly insurmountable unless totally new physics becomes available.

3.2 Quantum Teleportation

It turns out that there does in fact exist a form of teleportation that occurs in nature despite the numerous technical roadblocks described in the previous section. It is called *quantum teleportation*, which is based on the well-known concept of quantum entanglement. Erwin Schrödinger coined the word "entanglement" in 1935 in a three-part paper (Schrödinger, 1935a, b, c, 1980). These papers were prompted by the Einstein, Podolsky and Rosen (1935; denoted hereafter as EPR) paper that raised fundamental questions about quantum mechanics, whereby Einstein had loudly complained that quantum mechanics allowed physical processes resembling "spooky action at a distance" to occur. EPR recognized that quantum theory allows certain correlations to exist between two physically distant parts of a quantum system. Such correlations make it possible to predict the result of a measurement on one part of a system by looking at the distant part. On this basis, EPR argued that the distant predicted quantity

TELEPORTATION

should have a definite value even before being measured, if quantum theory is complete and respects locality (a.k.a. causality). EPR concluded that, from a classical perspective, quantum theory must be incomplete because it disallows such definite values prior to measurement. Schrödinger's perspective on this argument gives the modern view of quantum mechanics, which is to say that the wavefunction (a.k.a. quantum state vector) provides all the information there is about a quantum system. In regards to the nature of entangled quantum states, Schrödinger (1935a, b, c, 1980) stated that, "The whole is in a definite state, the parts taken individually are not." This statement defines the essence of pure-state entanglement. Schrödinger went on to give a description of quantum entanglement by introducing his famous cat experiment.

To better understand the concept of quantum entanglement/teleportation we will focus on the quantum wavefunction (a.k.a. quantum state function). Any quantum system such as a particle that possesses a position in space, energy, angular and linear momentum, and spin is completely described by a wavefunction. This is usually symbolized in a variety of ways, and we choose to represent a generic wavefunction using the traditional "bra-ket" notation of quantum mechanics: $|\varphi\rangle$. Anything that we want to know about the particle is mathematically encoded within $|\varphi\rangle$. As we discussed in the previous section the wavefunction can never be completely known because there is no measurement that can determine it completely. The only exception to this is in the special case that the wavefunction has been prepared in some particular state or some member of a known basis group of states in advance. By measuring one of the properties of a quantum system, we can get a glimpse of the overall quantum state that is encoded within $|\varphi\rangle$. According to the quantum uncertainty principle the act of doing such a measurement will destroy any ability to subsequently determine the other properties of the quantum system. So the act of measuring a particle actually destroys some of the information about its pristine state. This makes it impossible to copy particles and reproduce them elsewhere via quantum teleportation. However, it turns out that one can recreate an unmeasured quantum state in another particle as long as one is prepared to sacrifice the original particle. The trick is to exploit the EPR process to circumvent the quantum uncertainty principle.

As discussed previously, EPR discovered that a pair of spatially separated quantum sub-systems that are parts of an overall quantum system can be "entangled" in a non-local (i.e., non-causal) way. When two particles come into contact with one another, they can become "entangled." In an entangled state, both particles remain part of the same quantum system so that whatever you do to one of them affects the other one in a predictable fashion. More precisely, a measurement on one of the entangled sub-systems puts it into a particular quantum state, while instantaneously putting the sub-system with which it is entangled into a corresponding quantum state, while the two sub-systems are separated by arbitrarily large distances in spacetime (even backwards in time!). A simple example of this phenomenon is to prepare a pair of photons in the same quantum state such that they are entangled, and then allow them to fly apart to remote locations without any form of communication occurring between them along their journey. Measuring the polarization of one of the pair of entangled photons induces the other photon, which may be light-years away, into the same state of polarization as that which was measured for its entangled twin. The basic operation of quantum teleportation can be described as determining the total quantum state of some large quantum system, transmitting this state information from one place to another, and making a perfect reconstruction of the system at the new location. In principle, entangled particles can serve as "transporters" of sorts. By introducing a third "message" particle to one of the entangled particles, one could transfer its properties to the other one, without ever measuring those properties.

Historically, quantum entanglement was never reconciled with the quantum uncertainty principle and the requirement of locality (or causality) in observed physical phenomena, thus it became a paradox in quantum theory. A three-decade debate began following the appearance of the EPR paper over whether quantum entanglement (a.k.a. "spooky action at a distance") was a real quantum phenomenon or not, and this debate came to be called the "EPR dilemma." Einstein's only solution to the dilemma was to suggest that quantum mechanics was incomplete and needed a reformulation to incorporate local hidden-variables that can account for observed physical phenomena without violating causality. Bell (1964) later solved the EPR dilemma by deriving correlation inequalities that can be violated in quantum mechanics but have to be satisfied within every model that is local and complete. Such models are called "local hidden-variable models." Bell showed that a pair of entangled particles, which were once in contact but later moved too far apart to interact directly (i.e., causally), can exhibit individually random behavior that is too strongly correlated to be explained by classical statistics. Bell's inequalities make it possible to test whether local hidden-variable models can account for observed physical phenomena in lab experiments. Groundbreaking experimental work by Aspect et al. (1982a, b) along with further theoretical and experimental work done by others (Freedman and Clauser, 1972; Aspect, 1983; Aspect and Grangier, 1985; Hong and Mandel, 1985; Bennett and Wiesner, 1992; Tittel et al., 1998a, b; Tittel and Weihs, 2001) demonstrated violations of the Bell inequalities, which therefore invalidated the local hidden-variable models. The key result of recent theoretical and experimental work is that an observed violation of a Bell inequality demonstrates the presence of entanglement in a quantum system.

3.2.1 Description of the q-Teleportation Process

The experimental work of Bennett et al. (1993) followed by the theoretical and experimental work of others (Vaidman, 1994; Kwiat et al., 1995; Braunstein, 1996; Braunstein and Kimble, 1998; Pan et al., 1998; Stenholm and Bardroff, 1998; Zubairy, 1998; Vaidman and Yoran, 1999; Kwiat et al., 1999) made the breakthrough that was necessary to demonstrate the principle of quantum teleportation in practice. It was a remarkable technical breakthrough that settled, once and for all, the nagging question of whether quantum entanglement could be used to implement a teleportation process to transfer information between remotely distant quantum systems non-causally (i.e., at FTL speed). It is easy to describe how quantum teleportation works in greater detail. Figure 6 compares conventional facsimile transmission with the quantum teleportation process seen in Figure 7. In a conventional facsimile transmission the original document is scanned, extracting partial information about it, but it remains more or less intact after the scanning process. The scanned information is then sent to the receiving station, where it is imprinted on new paper to produce an approximate copy of the original. In quantum teleportation (Figure 7) one scans out part of the information from object A (the original), which one wants to teleport, while causing the remaining, unscanned, part of the information in A to pass, via EPR entanglement, into another object C which has never been in contact with A. Two objects B and C are prepared and brought into contact (i.e., entangled), and then separated. Object B is taken to the sending station, while object C is taken to the receiving station. At the sending station object B is scanned together with the original object A, yielding some information and totally disrupting the states of A and B. This scanned information is sent to the receiving station, where it is used to select one of several treatments to be applied to object C, thereby putting C into an exact replica of the former state of A. Object A itself is no longer in its original initial state, having been completely disrupted by the scanning process. The process just described is teleportation and not replication, and one should not confuse the two. There is a subtle, unscannable kind of information that, unlike ordinary information or material, can be delivered via EPR correlations/entanglement, such that it cannot by itself deliver a meaningful and controllable message. But quantum teleportation delivers exactly that part of the information in an object that is too delicate to be scanned out and delivered by conventional methods.

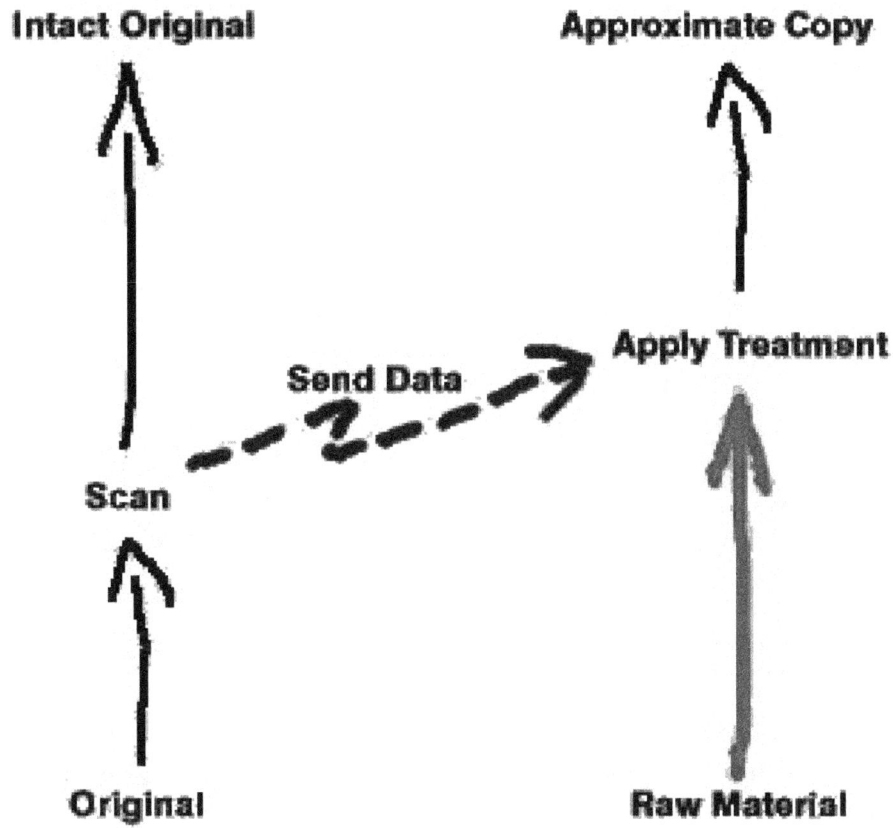

Figure 6. Classical Facsimile Transmission (Modified IBM Press Image)

TELEPORTATION

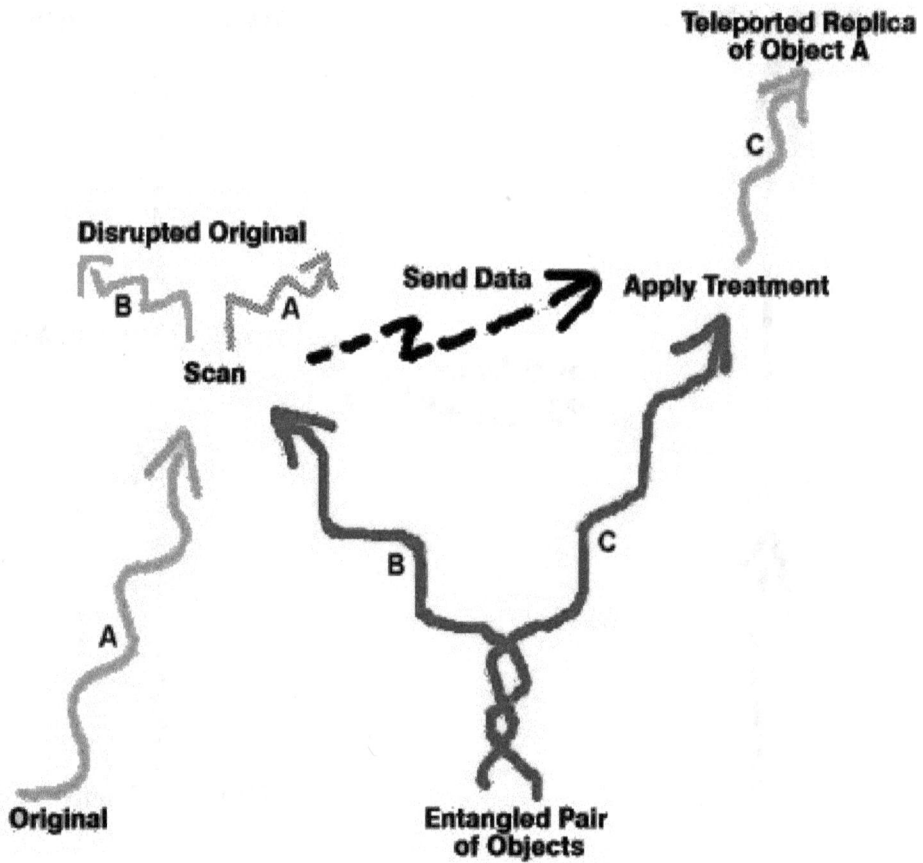

Figure 7. Quantum Teleportation (Modified IBM Press Image)

TELEPORTATION

We now go one more final step to give a simplified outline of the actual teleportation process according to Bennett et al. (1993). They propose a multistep procedure by which any quantum state $|\chi\rangle$ of a particle or a photon (that correspond to an N-state system) is to be teleported from one location to another. For example, $|\chi\rangle$ might be a two-level system that could refer to the polarization of a single photon, the nuclear magnetic spin of a hydrogen atom, or the electronic excitation of an effective two-level atom. The following scenario outlines the q-Teleportation process in a very simplified way:

1. Prepare a pair of quantum subsystems $|\varphi\rangle$ and $|\psi\rangle$ in an EPR entangled state so that they are linked together. $|\varphi\rangle$ and $|\psi\rangle$ are maximally entangled and together constitute a definite pure state superposition even though each of them is maximally undetermined or mixed when considered separately.

2. Transport $|\varphi\rangle$ to the location of the teleportation transmitter and transport $|\psi\rangle$ to the location of the teleportation receiver. (In the technical literature the transmitter is called "Alice" and the receiver is called "Bob.") The transmitter and receiver can be many light years apart in space. Note that the two subsystems are non-causally correlated via entanglement, but they contain no information about $|\chi\rangle$ at this point. The two subsystems represent an open quantum channel that is ready to transmit information.

3. Now Alice brings the teleported state $|\chi\rangle$ into contact with the entangled state $|\varphi\rangle$ and performs a quantum measurement on the combined system $|\chi\rangle|\varphi\rangle$. Bob and Alice have previously agreed upon the details of the quantum measurement.

4. Using a conventional classical communication channel, Alice transmits to Bob a complete description of the outcome of the quantum measurement she performed on $|\chi\rangle|\varphi\rangle$.

5. Bob then subjects $|\psi\rangle$ to a set of linear transformations (i.e., suitable unitary rotations) that are dictated by the outcome of Alice's quantum measurement. The quantum subsystem Bob originally first received is no longer in state $|\psi\rangle$ after the linear transformations because it is now in a state identical to the original state $|\chi\rangle$. Therefore, $|\chi\rangle$ has in effect been teleported from Alice to Bob.

Bennett et al. (1993) showed in their experimental work that this scheme requires both a conventional communication channel and a non-causal EPR channel to send the state $|\chi\rangle$ from one location to another. In addition to this, a considerable pre-arrangement of entangled states and quantum measurement procedures is required to make the process work. Bennett et al. (1993) analyzed the information flow implicit in the process and showed that Alice's measurement does not provide any information about the quantum state $|\chi\rangle$. All of the quantum state information is passed by the EPR link between the entangled particle states $|\varphi\rangle$ and $|\psi\rangle$. We can think of the measurement results as providing the "code key" that permits the EPR information to be decoded properly at Bob's end. And because the measurement information must travel on a conventional communications channel, the decoding cannot take place until the code key arrives, insuring that no FTL teleportation is possible.

The q-Teleportation scheme teleports the state of a quantum system without having to completely measure its initial state. The outcome of the process is that the initial quantum state $|\chi\rangle$ is destroyed at Alice's location and recreated at Bob's location. It is very important for the reader to understand that it is the _quantum states_ of the particles/photons that are destroyed and recreated in the teleportation process, and not the particles/photons themselves. The quantum state or wavefunction contains the information on the state of a particle, but is not a directly observable physical quantity like mass-energy. The quantum information contained within a state is available in the form of probabilities or expectation values.

TELEPORTATION

Therefore, q-Teleportation _cannot_ teleport animate or inanimate matter (or energy) in its physical entirety. However, some experts argue that because a particle's or a photon's quantum state is its defining characteristic, teleporting its quantum state is completely _equivalent_ to teleporting the particle/photon even though the original particle's/photon's quantum state (and defining characteristic) was completely destroyed in the process (more on this in Section 3.3). Therefore, no quantum cloning is possible and we are left with a (near-perfect) copy of the now-destroyed original after teleportation (Wootters and Zurek, 1982; Barnum et al., 1996). And finally, classical information itself _cannot_ be teleported faster than the speed of light via the non-causal EPR channel; however, quantum information can (more on this in Section 3.2.3).

3.2.2 Decoherence Fundamentally Limits q-Teleportation

Finally, the reader must understand that the q-Teleportation scenario described in the previous section was simplified because we unrealistically assumed that Alice and Bob shared an EPR entangled pair that was free of noise or decoherence. Decoherence is the process, whereby an object's quantum states degrade when information leaks to or from the environment (i.e., environmental noise) through stray interactions with the object. In reality, Alice and Bob have quantum systems that interact directly or through another mediating quantum system like two ions in an ion trap that interact through phonon modes of the trap, or Rydberg atoms in a laser cavity that interact via photons (Sackett, 2001; Raimond et al., 2001). Decoherence degrades the fidelity of the quantum link (i.e., the set of pure EPR entangled pairs) between two quantum systems, thus introducing a certain level of error in the exchange of quantum information between the systems.

In a real-world example of an application of q-Teleportation to quantum computation (discussed in the next section), we can devise an array of interconnected ion traps with each trap holding a small number of ions that are coupled by ions that are moved between the traps or by traveling photons (Wineland et al., 2002). The quantum link (or EPR interaction) between a pair of systems is subject to noise or decoherence through photon loss or heating of the phonons. At present, decoherence imposes a fundamental limit on our ability to perform quantum information processing. Research is continuing on whether decoherence can be reduced, circumvented, or otherwise be (partially or totally) eliminated. Dür and Briegel (2003) have taken the first step towards this goal at rudimentary level by showing that fault-tolerant quantum computation can be achieved in the presence of very high noise levels occurring in the interaction link between small quantum systems, if one assumes that local quantum processing on each end is nearly error free. They showed that the interaction link can have an error rate of two-thirds.

3.2.3 Recent Developments in Entanglement and q-Teleportation Physics

Quantum teleportation physics is still in its infancy. Both theoretical and experimental developments are advancing in many different directions, but are far from maturity at this point in time because the field is still evolving at present. Technical applications of entanglement and q-Teleportation are just becoming conceptualized for the first time, while a small number of basic physics breakthroughs and their related applications are in experimental progress at present. The research community is still in the process of discovering the full nature of entanglement and q-Teleportation, its rules, and what roadblocks nature has in store for its applications and further progression. The literature cited in this study is by no means complete, and only represents a subset of the entire field, because the research is still evolving.

An important application of quantum entanglement and q-Teleportation was the discovery made by Shor (1994, 1997) that computation with quantum states instead of classical bits can result in large savings in computation time. For example, the best algorithms take exponentially more resources to factor ever-larger numbers on a classical computer. A 500-digit number needs 10^8 times as many computational steps to factor as a 250-digit number. The latter classically requires $\approx 5\times10^{24}$ computational steps, or about 150,000 years computing time at terahertz speed, to factor. Shor found a polynomial-time quantum algorithm that solves the problem of finding prime factors of a large integer.

TELEPORTATION

He showed that his algorithm rises only polynomially so that a 500-digit number takes only eight times as many computational steps to factor as a 250-digit number. And by using the quantum factoring algorithm, a 250-digit number requires only $\approx 5 \times 10^{10}$ steps or < 1 second to factor at terahertz speed, so that a 500-digit number will take ≤ 1 second to factor. No classical polynomial-time algorithm for this problem exists at present. This breakthrough generated a cottage industry of research into quantum computing and quantum information theory.

IBM (2001) constructed a prototype quantum computer that uses the nuclear spins of seven atoms that are part of a large molecule with the iron-based chemical composition $H_5C_{11}O_2F_5Fe$. The computer uses entangled nuclear spins for storage and has a capacity of seven qubits (qubits are defined in the bulleted list in the next two paragraphs below). All of the Fluorine atoms in the large molecule are Fluorine isotope 19 and two of the Carbon atoms are Carbon isotope 13. All the other non-hydrogen atoms have even isotope numbers and no nuclear spins. The objective of the prototype quantum computer was to factor the number 15 into its two prime factors 3 and 5 by using Shor's quantum factoring algorithm. The quantum computation required that a sample of $\approx 10^{18}$ of the large molecules be placed in a magnetic field and manipulated by nuclear magnetic resonance (NMR) techniques. This mechanism allows the spins to function as qubits, whereby Schor's algorithm can be performed via manipulation of the NMR fields. NMR was used to implement quantum computing in this prototype, because the nuclear spins are well isolated from decoherence as a result of the very long decoherence time (the time after which quantum coherence is lost due to environmental noise) in the system.

To factor larger numbers will require a system that uses more than seven qubits. It is estimated that a quantum computer using ≈ 36 qubits could very quickly perform computations that would require a conventional computer ≈ 13 billion years to perform. And such a computer could solve one of the technical problems of human teleportation discussed in Section 3.1. However, a scale-up in the number of qubits is difficult because the IBM prototype has reached the technology limit of NMR quantum computing. The prototype's operation requires that all of the qubits must be in the same molecule. And molecules with more than seven spins that can be used as qubits are not feasible at present. However, there are alternative technologies for quantum computing that show promise for scaling up the number of qubits. The technologies of nuclear spin orientation of single atom impurities in semiconductors, electron spin orientation in quantum dots, and the manipulation of magnetic flux quanta in superconductors all show promise of providing a basis for scalable quantum computers. Finally, the primary technical problem in quantum computing at the present time is decoherence, and this must be eliminated or otherwise mitigated before new quantum technology can become competitive with conventional computer technology.

A byproduct of the recent quantum computing and information research is that a modern theory of entanglement has emerged. Researchers now treat entanglement as a quantifiable physical resource that enables quantum information processing and computation. Entanglement is no longer treated as a paradox of quantum theory. It has been recently discovered that (Nielsen and Chuang, 2000; Nielsen, 2003; Terhal et al., 2003):

- various kinds of pure and mixed entangled states may be prepared in addition to the simple pure-state superpositions that was described in the previous section

- the members of an entangled group of objects do not have their own individual quantum states, only the group as a whole has a well-defined state (i.e., "the whole is greater than the sum of its parts")

- entangled objects behave as if they were physically connected together no matter how far apart they actually are, distance does not attenuate entanglement in the slightest – it has been demonstrated that information can be teleported over 40 km using existing technology (H. Everitt, Army Research Office, 2000)

TELEPORTATION

- if something is entangled with other objects, then a measurement of it simultaneously provides information about its partners

- some quantum systems can have a little entanglement while others will have a lot

- the more entanglement available, the better suited a system is to quantum information processing

- decoherence degrades the fidelity of the quantum link (i.e., the set of pure EPR entangled pairs) between two quantum systems, thus introducing a certain level of error in the exchange of quantum information between the systems; thus limiting our ability to perform quantum information processing (see more on this issue in the next paragraph below)

- mixed entangled states may be measured, distilled, concentrated, diluted, and manipulated

- the basic resource of classical information is the bit (i.e., the two values 0 and 1), while quantum information comes in quantum bits (i.e., qubits) that are described by their quantum state; qubits can exist in superpositions that simultaneously involve 0 and 1, thus giving them an infinite range of values; groups of qubits can be entangled; qubits must be insulated against decoherence, so that the coherent state of the quantum system in a quantum computer is preserved for a time that is long enough to set up a calculation, perform it, and read out the results

- quantum computers processing qubits or entangled qubits can outperform classical computers; functional requirements of quantum computers:

    ❖ they must have the ability to initialize any qubit in a specified state, and to measure the state of a specific qubit
    ❖ they must have universal quantum gates, which are logical elements capable of arranging any desired logical relationship between the states of qubits
    ❖ they must also have a processor capable of interlinking quantum gates to establish rules and boundary conditions for their inter-relationships – in a quantum computation, the arrangement of quantum gates connects the qubits in a logical pattern, according to a program or algorithm, and after an interval the qubits assigned to the result are read out

- quantum error correction codes exist, whereby qubits are passed through a circuit (the quantum analogue of logic gates) that will successfully fix an error in any one of the qubits without actually reading what all the individual qubit states are; no qubit cloning is required

- a completely secure quantum key can be generated and distributed (for communication and decoding of encrypted messages) using entangled photons has been demonstrated (Tittel et al., 2000; Jennewein et al., 2000; Naik et al., 2000); any eavesdropper's attempt to intercept the quantum key will alter the contents in a detectable way, enabling users to discard the compromised parts of the data

- in an experiment which verified that EPR entanglement obeys Special Relativity (Seife, 2000; Scarani et al., 2000; Gisin et al., 2000; Zbinden et al., 2000a, b), and involving a photon detector moving at relativistic speeds (for example, Bob moves away from Alice at close to the speed of light), investigators determined that quantum information via EPR photon pair entanglement must travel $> 10^7$ times light speed (the photon detectors were 10.6 km apart)

TELEPORTATION

- investigators are still developing quantitative laws of entanglement to provide a set of principles for understanding the behavior of entanglement and how it is used to do information processing

- investigators are working to develop an understanding of the general principles that govern complex quantum systems such as quantum computers

Other developments are equally as interesting or compelling. For example, the quantum state of the object we wish to teleport does not have to describe single microscopic systems like photons, ions, atoms or electrons. Quantum states can describe large collections of atoms like chemical compounds, humans, planets, stars, and galaxies. Hartle and Hawking (1983) even derived the quantum wavefunction of the Universe in closed form, although, it was extremely simplified and excluded the presence of quantum matter-energy. So it has become possible to consider teleporting large quantum systems. We summarize the more recent spectacular developments in the following:

- <u>Generation of entanglement and teleportation by Parametric Down-Conversion (Bouwmeester et al., 1997; Zeilinger, 2003)</u>: EPR entangled photon pairs are created when a laser beam passes through a nonlinear β-barium borate or BBO crystal. Inside the crystal (BBO, for example) an ultraviolet photon (λ = 490 nm) may spontaneously split into two lower energy infrared photons (λ = 780 nm), which is called parametric down-conversion. The two "down-conversion" photons emerge as independent beams with orthogonal polarizations (horizontal or vertical). (The orthogonal polarization states represent a classic example of the discrete quantum state variables that can be teleported. Other examples of discrete quantum variables that have been teleported using other schemes include the nuclear magnetic spin of a hydrogen atom, electronic excitations of an effective two-level atom, elementary particle spins, etc.) In the two beams along the intersections of their emission cones, we observe a polarization-entangled two-photon state. For the experimental realization of quantum teleportation, it is necessary to use pulsed down-conversion. Only if the pulse width of the UV light, and thus the time of generating photon pairs is shorter than the coherence time of the down-converted photons, then interferometric Bell-state analysis can be performed. In this type of experiment, the pulses from a mode-locked Ti:Saphire laser have been frequency doubled to give pulses of $\approx$ 200 fs duration (1 fs = 10^{-15} second). The interfering light is observed after passage through IR filters of 4 nm bandwidth giving a coherence time of $\approx$ 520 fs. After retroflection during its second passage through the crystal, the UV pulse creates another pair of photons. One of these will be the teleported photon, which can be prepared to have any polarization. Beam splitters and photon detectors are used to perform the Bell-state analysis during the standard teleportation process that ensues. See Figure 8 for a schematic showing the layout of a standard parametric down-conversion entanglement-teleportation experiment.

- <u>Teleportation of squeezed states of light and continuous quantum state variables (Furusawa et al., 1998; Sørensen, 1998; Braunstein and Kimble, 1998; Opatrný et al., 2000, Braunstein et al., 2001; Zhang et al., 2002; Bowen et al., 2002; Bowen et al., 2003; Zeilinger, 2003)</u>: Squeezed light (see Section A.2 in Appendix A) is used to generate the EPR entangled beams, which are sent to Alice and Bob. A third beam, the input, is a coherent state of unknown complex amplitude. This state is teleported to Bob with a high fidelity only achievable via the use of quantum entanglement. Entangled EPR beams are generated by combining two beams of squeezed light at a 50/50 beam splitter. EPR beam 1 propagates to Alice's sending station, where it is combined at a 50/50 beam splitter with the unknown input state, in this case a coherent state of unknown complex amplitude. Alice uses two sets of balanced homodyne detectors to make a Bell-state measurement on the amplitudes of the combined state. Because of the entanglement between the EPR beams, Alice's detection collapses Bob's field (EPR beam 2) into a state

TELEPORTATION

conditioned on Alice's measurement outcome. After receiving the classical result from Alice, Bob is able to construct the teleported state via a simple phase-space displacement of the EPR field 2. Quantum teleportation in this scheme is theoretically perfect, yielding an output state which equals the input with a fidelity $F = 1$. In practice, fidelities less than one are realized due to imperfections in the EPR pair, Alice's Bell measurement, and Bob's unitary transformation. By contrast, a sender and receiver who share only a classical communication channel cannot hope to transfer an arbitrary quantum state with a fidelity of one. For coherent states, the classical teleportation limit is $F = 0.5$, while for light polarization states it is $F = 0.67$. The quantum nature of the teleportation achieved in this case is demonstrated by the experimentally determined fidelity of $F = 0.58$, greater than the classical limit of 0.5 for coherent states. The fidelity is an average over all input states and so measures the ability to transfer an arbitrary, unknown superposition from Alice to Bob. This technique achieves the teleportation of continuous quantum state variables, as opposed to the discrete quantum state variables used in the Bennett et al. (1993) teleportation protocol and its variants. The teleportation of a squeezed state of light from one beam of light to another demonstrates the teleportation of a continuous feature (of light) that comes from the superpositions of an infinite number of basic states of the electromagnetic field, such as those found in squeezed states. This line of research also involves the experimental demonstration of the mapping of quantum states from photonic to atomic media via entanglement and teleportation. Hald et al. (1999) reported on the experimental observation of a spin-squeezed macroscopic ensemble of 10^7 cold atoms, whereby the ensemble is generated via quantum state entanglement/teleportation from non-classical light to atoms.

TELEPORTATION

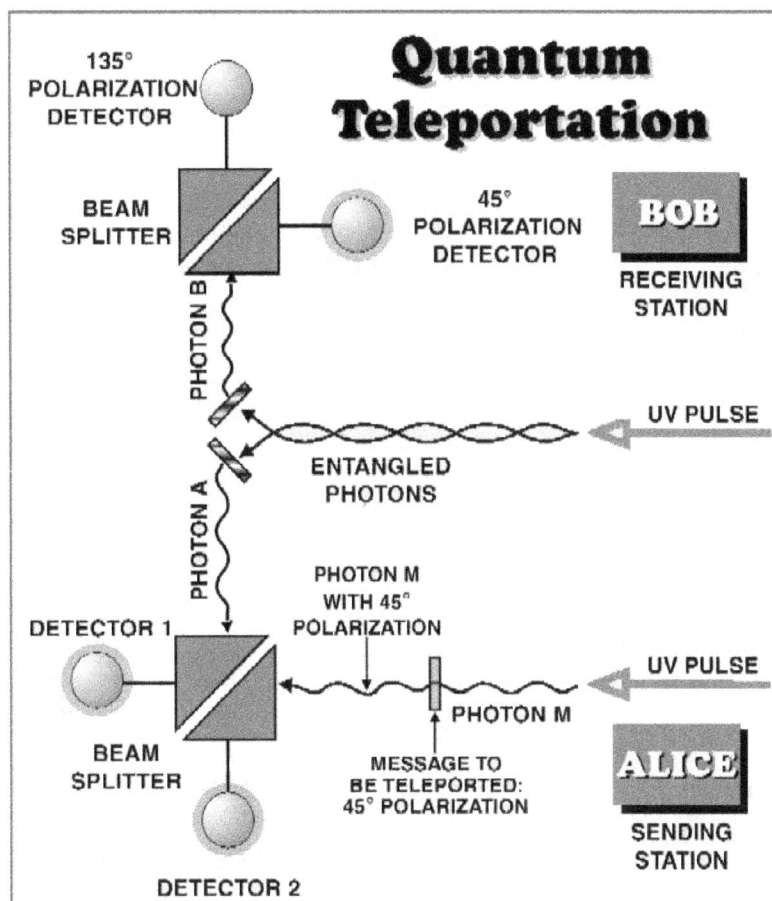

Figure 8. Quantum Teleportation (From www.aip.org)

At the sending station of the quantum teleporter, Alice encodes a "messenger" photon (M) with a specific state: 45 degrees polarization. This travels towards a beam splitter. Meanwhile, two additional entangled photons (A and B) are created. The polarization of each photon is in a fuzzy, undetermined state, yet the two photons have a precisely defined interrelationship. Specifically, they must have complementary polarizations. For example, if photon A is later measured to have horizontal (0 degrees) polarization, then the other photon must collapse into the complementary state of vertical (90 degrees) polarization. Entangled photon A arrives at the beam splitter at the same time as the message photon M. The beam splitter causes each photon to either continue toward detector 1 or change course and travel to detector 2. In 25% of all cases, in which the two photons go off into different detectors, Alice does not know which photon went to which detector. This inability for Alice to distinguish between the two photons causes quantum weirdness to kick in. Just by the very fact that the two photons are now indistinguishable, the M photon loses its original identity and becomes entangled with A. The polarization value for each photon is now indeterminate, but since they travel toward different detectors Alice knows that the two photons must have complementary polarizations. Since message photon M must have complementary polarization to photon A, then the other entangled photon (B) must now attain the same polarization value as M. Therefore, teleportation is successful. Indeed, Bob sees that the polarization value of photon B is 45 degrees: the initial value of the message photon.

TELEPORTATION

- <u>Entanglement of Atoms (Hagley et al., 1997; Sackett et al., 2000)</u>: EPR entanglement at the level of atoms has been experimentally demonstrated using rubidium atoms prepared in circular Rydberg states (i.e., the outer electrons of the atom have been excited to very high energy states and are far from the nucleus in circular orbits). The experimental apparatus produces two entangled atoms, one atom in a ground state and the other atom in an excited state, physically separated so that the entanglement is non-local. And when a measurement is made on one atom, let us say the atom in a ground state, then the other atom instantaneously presents itself in the excited state – the result of the second atom wave function collapse, thus determined by the result of the first atom wave function collapse. This work is now evolving towards the demonstration of entanglement for molecules and larger entities followed by teleportation of their states. Bose and Home (2002) have improved on this concept by proposing a single, simple generic method by which any atoms, ions and macroscopic objects can be entangled and teleported.

- <u>Teleportation of an Atomic State via Cavity Decay (Bose et al., 1999; Sackett et al., 2000)</u>: It has been shown how the state of an atom trapped in a cavity can be teleported to a second atom trapped in a distant cavity simply by detecting photon decays from the cavities.

- <u>Biological Quantum Teleportation (Mavromatos et al., 2002)</u>: There are several obstacles to teleporting large complicated objects, especially biological entities. Decoherence is the primary obstacle. That is because observable quantum effects in biological matter is thought to be strongly suppressed due to the macroscopic nature of most biological entities and the fact that such systems live at near room temperature, and there is always contact between biological entities and the environment (the source of decoherence). These conditions result in very fast collapse of pertinent quantum wavefunctions to one of the allowed classical states of the biological entity. Mavromatos et al. (2002) propose a daring model that predicts dissipationless energy transfer along shielded macromolecules at near room temperatures as well as quantum teleportation of states across microtubules and perhaps neurons. It is proposed that under certain circumstances it is in principle possible to obtain the necessary isolation against environmental decoherence, so that meso/macroscopic quantum coherence, and entanglement extending over scales that are larger than the atomic scale, may be achieved and maintained for times comparable to the characteristic times for biological and cellular processes. Microtubules are comprised of tubulin that is a common polar protein found in the cytoskeleton of eukaryotic cells, which is especially enriched in brain tissue. The model treats microtubules as quantum mechanically isolated high-Q QED cavities, exhibiting properties analogous to those of electromagnetic cavities routinely used in quantum optics. The model builds a microtubule network that achieves quantum teleportation of coherent quantum states, leading to decoherence-resistant bulk quantum information processing and computing within the biological matter. It is speculated that the model can explain how consciousness works, and how the brain processes and computes information.

- <u>Teleportation of a laser beam with embedded radio signal (Bowen et al., 2003)</u>: The teleportation of a laser beam from one part of a lab to another has been demonstrated. Investigators embedded a radio signal into a laser beam, then disintegrated the beam and reassembled it a meter away, virtually instantaneously. The laser beam was destroyed in the teleportation process, but the radio signal survived. The laser light at one end of an optical communications system was disassembled and its replica was recreated elsewhere in the lab. Even though the laser beam did not survive teleportation, its encoded message did. This system could be used to transport secure data, such that it could become possible to construct a perfect cryptography system. When two

TELEPORTATION

parties want to communicate with one another, one can enable the secrecy of the communication to be absolutely perfect.

- Entanglement and Teleportation of a Macroscopic Ensemble of Atoms (Julsgaard et al., 2001): Expanding upon the earlier work of Hald et al. (1999) and Sackett et al. (2000), investigators experimentally demonstrated the entanglement of two macroscopic objects, each consisting of a cesium gas sample containing $\approx 10^{12}$ atoms. Entanglement is generated via interaction of the samples with a pulse of light, which performs a non-local Bell measurement on the collective spins of the samples. The entangled spin-state can be maintained for 0.5 milliseconds. The teleportation of macro-ensemble atom quantum states is expected to follow this experiment. This work is evolving towards the experimental demonstration of the Bose and Home (2002) proposal, which proved that there is a single generic process that can entangle and teleport any atoms, ions and macroscopic objects.

- Entanglement/teleportation of internal state and external motion information of atoms (Opatrný and Kurizki, 2001): Investigators propose an experiment for transmitting an atom's full information, including its "external" states, such as its energy of motion. This procedure replicates the quantum features of the external motion of a particle. For example, if particle-to-be-teleported C yielded a diffraction pattern after passing through two slits, then the same pattern would be produced by particle B, which receives the teleported information. The researchers propose the following idea: Dissociate a very cold molecule with a laser pulse into two atoms (called A and B). Then manipulate the two atoms so that they become entangled: each one is in a fuzzy state individually, but has a precisely defined relationship with its partner. Then let one of the entangled particles (such as A) collide with particle C, whose unknown state should be teleported. After their collision, the momentum values of the collision partners A and C are measured. With that information, the researchers know how to "kick" and deflect atom B, so that the motion of B precisely emulates that of particle C. The investigators say that state-of-the-art equipment for studying atomic collisions and quantum effects makes this experiment difficult, but feasible, to do. If this proposal proves to be correct, then the implication is that it will become possible to experimentally expand this concept to the teleportation of a large ensemble of atoms, such that the entire physical motion and quantum states of the ensemble can be teleported. This could lead to the future development of a teleportation process similar to what was discussed in Section 3.1.

- Laser-like Amplification of Entangled Particles and Entangled-Photon Lasers (Lamas-Linares et al., 2001): Entangled particles are notoriously difficult to create in bulk. To create entangled photons, for example, researchers use the parametric down-conversion technique to send laser light through a barium borate crystal. Passing through the crystal, a photon sometimes splits into two entangled photons (each with half the energy of the initial photon). However, this only occurs for one in every ten billion incoming photons. To increase the yield, researchers added a step: they put mirrors beyond the crystal so that the laser pulse and entangled pair could reflect, and have the chance to interact. The entangled pair and reflected laser pulse interfere constructively to generate fourfold more two-photon pairs or interfere destructively to create zero pairs. Following these steps, the researchers increased production of two-photon entangled pairs, and also of more rare states such as four-photon entangled quartets. This achievement could represent a step towards an entangled-photon laser, which would repeatedly amplify entangled particles to create greater yields than previously possible, and also towards the creation of new and more complex kinds of entangled states.

This list is by no means complete as new developments in this field continue to arise.

TELEPORTATION

3.3 Conclusion and Recommendations

Given the incredible advancements that have been made in the entanglement and teleportation of macroscopic objects the size of 10^{12} atoms, we are still very far away from being able to entangle and teleport human beings (and even simpler biological entities such as cells, etc.) and bulk inanimate objects (tools, technical equipment, pencils and pens, weapons platforms, communications devices, personal hygiene supplies, etc.). There still remain four essential problems:

➢ One needs an entangled pair of such bulk objects.

➢ The bulk objects to be entangled and teleported must be in a pure quantum state (as in a Bose-Einstein condensate, for example). And pure quantum states are very fragile.

➢ The bulk objects to be entangled and teleported must be extremely isolated from the environment to prevent the onset of decoherence.

➢ The Bell-state measurement of animate or inanimate objects during entanglement/teleportation will require extracting an amount of information (in bits) that equals or exceeds the number of atoms contained within the object. This infers that the computer storage and processing requirements to entangle and teleport a complete bulk object will be astronomically huge (recall the discussion in Section 3.1).

It is difficult to imagine how we can achieve an extreme level of environmental isolation for an object, let alone a living being that breathes air and radiates heat. Experiments with atoms and larger objects must be done in a high vacuum to avoid collisions with molecules. Thermal radiation from the walls of a teleportation apparatus would easily disturb a tiny amount of matter. At present, decoherence imposes a fundamental limit on quantum entanglement and teleportation. Decoherence is the primary reason why we do not routinely see any quantum effects in our everyday world. Research is continuing on whether decoherence can be reduced, circumvented, or otherwise be eliminated. And some minor progress has been made in that direction.

In q-Teleportation it is the _quantum states_ of the objects that are destroyed and recreated, and not the objects themselves. Therefore, q-Teleportation _cannot_ teleport animate or inanimate matter (or energy) in its physical entirety. However, some experts argue that because an object's quantum state is its defining characteristic, teleporting its quantum state is completely _equivalent_ to teleporting the object, even though the original object's quantum state (and defining characteristic) was completely destroyed in the process. This goes to the heart of what is meant by identity. When an object has all the right properties and features, it will be the same object that one observes whether it was observed now or 24 hours ago. Quantum physics reinforces the point that objects of the same type in the same quantum state are indistinguishable from each other. One should, according to this quantum principle, be able to swap all the atoms in a particular object with the same atoms from a mound of raw materials, and reproduce the original object's quantum states exactly with the end result that the new object is identical to the original. Last, we do not know how to put a human being into a pure quantum state or what doing so would mean for biological functioning (including brain function), but we do know how to put $\leq 10^{12}$ gas atoms/ions and a beam of photons into a pure state in practice. Further research will be required to ascertain whether microbiological and higher-level biological systems, in addition to bulk inanimate matter, can be put into pure quantum states and entangled/teleported.

To perform a Bell-state measurement on (bulk) animate or inanimate objects, during the entanglement/teleportation process, to extract and encode its information will require extracting an amount of information (in bits) that equals or exceeds the number of atoms contained within the object. An object containing a few grams of matter will require the extraction of $> 10^{28}$ bits of data. A simple virus of $\approx 10^7$ atoms would require the extraction of $\geq 10^8$ bits of information during the entanglement/teleportation process, whereas the extraction of a minimum of 10^{28} kilobytes will be required to encode and store an entire human being. This is beyond the capability of present digital electronic computer technology to store and process. It is difficult to see how far computer technology will advance towards meeting this requirement.

It is difficult to fathom what will be in store for the teleportation of human beings given some possible future technology. What about the effects of the q-Teleportation process on the human consciousness, memories and dreams, and the spirit or soul? We know from quantum physics that "the whole is greater than the sum of its parts." So what happens to the fundamental characteristics of a human being when he/she steps into the teleporter-transmitter, where their quantum states (i.e., their complete identity) are destroyed during the quantum entanglement/teleportation process, and then their copy is created at the teleporter-receiver an instant later? What will things be like during the entanglement process? Will a teleported individual's consciousness, memories and dreams, and spirit/soul be successfully and accurately teleported or not? This is a major ethical and technical question that will have to be addressed by future research.

•**Recommendations**:

> **Broad-spectrum Quantum Computing Technology Development Program**: At present, the Quantum Information Science Program (QISP) is coordinated by the U.S. Army Research Office with funding and support from the Army, the National Security Agency, DARPA, and the Office of the Deputy Director of Defense for Research and Engineering. The Naval Research Lab and the CIA are both involved in their own programs. The CIA vets new commercial development of computer technology and computer information processing via its In-Q-Tel company (reference 44). This includes R&D on quantum entanglement and teleportation for computer, information processing and secure communications. QISP was funded for $19 million in 1999. The program involves 34 projects by researchers at 21 universities, three government laboratories and two corporate laboratories. QISP goals include building a quantum computer, developing quantum information processing, and further advances in quantum teleportation. The AFRL should join QISP and provide partnership funding on the order of $1 million per year. An alternative to this would be for AFRL to collaborate with In-Q-Tel and participate in its technology R&D venture capital programs. This R&D investment would allow the Air Force to acquire very advanced quantum physics and related technological applications that can support its mission. The R&D investment benefits would include the development and implementation of quantum computing/information processing and secured quantum communications technology, which can significantly enhance the performance and security of Air Force computing and communication systems infrastructure, and aerospace weapons systems.

> **Quantum Cryptography**: A dedicated research program should be implemented to develop a mature quantum cryptography technology. Theoretical and experimental work is in progress among a small number of select groups (QISP, In-Q-Tel, universities, etc.), but this field is not advancing fast enough for practical applications to become available to meet increasing adversarial threats against secured military and intelligence communications. The goal of proposed quantum cryptography research is to bring the theoretical and experimental foundation of quantum cryptography and secure quantum information processing to maturity, and to fully develop and implement quantum entanglement/teleportation-based cryptography technology. Recent experimental work has demonstrated that a completely secure quantum key can be generated and distributed for the communication and decoding of encrypted messages using entangled photons. Any eavesdropper's attempt to intercept the quantum key will alter the contents in a detectable way, enabling users to discard the compromised parts of the data. There is much more work that needs to be done in this area. I recommend that the AFRL implement a

TELEPORTATION

$1 million/year program for five years in order to advance the state-of-art in quantum cryptography technology.

> Quantum Decoherence: Decoherence is the primary reason why we do not routinely see any quantum effects in our everyday world. And it imposes a fundamental limit on quantum entanglement and teleportation via the interaction between entangled/teleported quantum systems and their local environment. In order to advance quantum entanglement/teleportation physics and develop applied technologies, it is necessary that a research program be implemented by the AFRL to explore whether decoherence can be significantly reduced, circumvented, or otherwise be eliminated. An insufficient number of small university groups have slowly made minor progress in this direction. I recommend that a $500,000 - 750,000 per year R&D program be conducted for five years to overcome this technical challenge.

> Pure Quantum States: In order to entangle and teleport quantum particles and bulk objects, they both must be prepared in a pure quantum state. And pure quantum states are very fragile to decoherence. A technical challenge for entanglement/teleportation physics is whether the requirement for pure quantum states can be relaxed and how much decoherence will play a role in this situation, what technical challenges will arise when increasing the size of entangled/teleported matter to larger macroscopic scale ($\gg 10^{12}$ atoms), and whether matter of mixed composition (such as a gas or Bose-Einstein condensate of mixed atomic elements) can be entangled/teleported in both pure and mixed quantum states. I recommend that a $250,000 – 500,000 per year research program be conducted for five years to study this problem.

> Entangling Bulk Matter and Bell-State Measurement to Extract Information: Recent experiments demonstrated the entanglement of two macroscopic objects, each consisting of a cesium gas sample containing $\approx 10^{12}$ atoms. Entanglement was generated via interaction of the samples with a pulse of light, which performs a non-local Bell measurement on the collective spins of the samples. In order to push the envelope on this development and take it to higher practical levels, it will be necessary to ascertain the limit on the size and composition of bulk matter entanglement (given the decoherence and pure-state constraints); and to determine what other quantum states can be used for entanglement, what other Bell-state measurement techniques can be used, and whether multiple quantum states can be entangled. The chief technical challenge is the computer technology that will be required to facilitate the huge amount of data that must be extracted, processed and stored from bulk matter quantum states during the Bell-state measurement process. I recommend that a $500,000 – 1 million per year research program be implemented for five years in order to explore these questions and ascertain what solutions may be technically available, and to develop such solutions.

> Biological Quantum Teleportation: The Mavromatos et al. (2002) theoretical model for biological entanglement and teleportation is a remarkable concept that could result in the development of a workable physics theory of consciousness. The model has potential applications to advanced quantum computing/information processing physics and the physics of psi phenomena (see Chapter 5). A research program should be implemented to continue the Mavromatos et al. (2002) work and bring their model to theoretical maturity. It is recommended that this program be funded at $500,000 – 800,000 per year for five years. A parallel or follow-up program should be implemented to experimentally test this model and ascertain any useful technological applications. One application that should be explored in the proposed research program is advanced, ultra-fast, ultra-high-capacity quantum computing and information processing using natural and/or artificial biological systems. The parallel or follow-up experimental research program should be funded at $800,000 – 1.5 million per year for five years.

TELEPORTATION

- FTL Communication: Experiments verifying that EPR entanglement obeys Special Relativity (Seife, 2000; Scarani et al., 2000; Gisin et al., 2000; Zbinden et al., 2000a, b) determined that quantum information via EPR photon pair entanglement must travel $> 10^7$ times light speed. Can this mechanism be exploited to achieve FTL communication? If so, then the potential military and commercial applications will be revolutionary, and the science and industry of communications will be forever transformed. A comprehensive theoretical and experimental research program should be implemented to answer this question. It is recommended that this program be funded at $700,000 – 1 million per year for five years. A modest experiment definition study should be funded at $80,000 for one year to delineate the most promising experimental approaches to be used for the larger research program. [There is much controversy and debate over FTL (a.k.a. superluminal) signals/communication, and the reader should see the selected superluminal references in the Teleportation References section of this study.]

- New Entanglement/Teleportation Breakthroughs: The most exciting developments in quantum teleportation physics has included the teleportation of a laser beam with an embedded radio signal, the teleportation of squeezed states of light (and hence, continuous quantum state variables), the teleportation of photon states to atoms/ions (from light to matter!), the entanglement of two similar/dissimilar quantum particles that are created by two (independently) different particle sources, the laser-like amplification of entangled particle/photon pairs, parametric down-conversion entanglement and teleportation (of discrete quantum state variables), quantum cryptography with unbreakable keys, the teleportation of quantum information at speeds $> 10^7$ times light speed, the entanglement and teleportation of macroscopic (10^{12} atoms) matter quantum states, etc. There is also the yet-untested proposal to entangle/teleport the external physical motion and internal quantum state information of atoms. This shows that quantum physics sets no apparent limit on what it is that can be teleported/entangled and how it is to be teleported/entangled, or where it is to be teleported/entangled. At present teleportation technology requires fiber optic and coaxial cables to teleport quantum state information from one location to another. Can we avoid the use of cables and teleport through free space? [Note: Before this report went to press, Aspelmeyer et al. (2003) reported their outdoor experiment that demonstrated the distribution of quantum entanglement (of laser photons) via optical free-space links to independent receivers separated by 600 m across the Danube River (during inclement nighttime weather), with no line of sight between them. This experiment is revolutionary and begins the step toward conducting satellite-based distributed quantum entanglement.] We have not discovered all the possibilities that nature has in store for us. The present breakthrough discoveries will likely introduce novel military and intelligence technology applications in the near and far future. But further R&D must be conducted in order to discover new applications for these recent breakthroughs, to make additional breakthroughs and discoveries, and to advance the state-of-art in quantum teleportation physics to meet future challenges to the Air Force mission. I recommend that a two-track R&D program be implemented over five years. The first track should be funded at $250,000 – 750,000 per year for the purpose of developing new entanglement/teleportation breakthroughs in quantum teleportation physics. The second track should be funded at $750,000 – 1.5 million per year for the purpose of developing applications for any new breakthroughs with the proviso that such applications benefit the Air Force mission and have commercial dual-use capability to leverage advance technology in the private sector.

TELEPORTATION

4.0 e-TELEPORTATION

4.1 Extra Space Dimensions and Parallel Universes/Spaces

A literature search for proposed e-Teleportation concepts based on the conveyance of objects through extra space dimensions and/or parallel universes/spaces has yielded only one result (see Section 4.2). The present state-of-art in research on parallel universes/spaces and extra space dimensions has been strictly limited to the work on developing a grand unified quantum field theory and a quantum theory of gravity, whereby the former necessarily includes the latter. Quantum gravity/unified field theory research has been evolving since the 1920s when Kaluza and Klein published the first papers to describe a model for the unification of gravity with electrodynamics. Many of the more prominent theories today invoke extra spatial dimensions, the existence of parallel universes/spaces, or both in order to quantise gravity and/or to unify gravity with the other forces of nature. It is beyond the scope of this study to provide an in-depth review of all of the research that has been done in this area, so we list below a select few of the historically prominent models that have largely gained a secure foothold in present-day research:

➢ Kaluza-Klein Electromagnetic-Gravity Unification Theory/Modern Kaluza-Klein Gravity Theories (Kaluza, 1921; Klein, 1926; de Sabbata and Schmutzer, 1983; Lee, 1984; Appelquist et al., 1987; Kaku, 1993, 1994; Overduin and Wesson, 1998): It was originally suggested that Maxwellian electrodynamics and Einstein gravitation could be unified in a theory of five-dimensional Riemannian geometry, where the gravitational and electromagnetic potentials together would determine the structure of spacetime. The fifth space dimension is curled up into a ball of space with a radius slightly larger than 10^{-35} m, and it was originally regarded as having no physical significance because it was simply a mathematical tool used to catalyze unification. At present, the generic name of Kaluza-Klein stands for a wide variety of approaches to quantising and unifying gravitation with other quantum fields using any number of dimensions greater than four.

➢ Superstring Theories (Green, 1985; Kaku, 1988, 1993, 1994): These theories come in a wide variety of interrelated concepts, and they are a highly evolved form of Kaluza-Klein theories. They are based on the dynamics of string-like fundamental quanta, whereby the observed fundamental particles are manifested by the vibrational ground or excitation states of a quantum string (open or closed loop). The superstrings are $\approx 10^{-35}$ m (i.e., the Planck length) in size. There are different versions of these theories that require ten, eleven or twenty-six extra space dimensions to unify and quantise gravity, whereby the extra dimensions are curled up (i.e., compactified) into balls of space with a radius $< 10^{-35}$ m. These theories later evolved into versions that are now called F- and M-theory. The mathematics behind this class of theories is very ugly, and it is difficult for even the best superstring theorists to make simple or sophisticated calculations and predictions. And so far, this class of quantum gravity theories has escaped experimental verification.

➢ D-Brane and 3-Brane Theories/Parallel Spaces (Rubakov and Shaposhnikov, 1983a, b; Polchinski, 1995; Antoniadis et al., 1998; Randall and Sundrum, 1999a, b; Weiss, 2000; Pease, 2001; Arkani-Hamed et al., 1998, 2000, 2002): D-brane theory is a recent incarnation of the original superstring theories in which open strings, corresponding to the fundamental particles of the standard model (quarks, leptons, gauge bosons), have their free ends stuck on a (hypersurface) membrane called a D-brane (D = Dirichlet boundary conditions). But the graviton, which corresponds to a closed loop of string, can propagate in all the dimensions. It provides both unification and quantization of gravity by assuming that there are n new spatial dimensions in addition to the three infinite spatial dimensions we know about. And the extra space dimensions are $\approx 10^{-35}$ m in extent. A very recent alternative version of this model is called "3-brane" theory. In this theory, each of the n extra space dimensions is of finite extent $R \approx 2 \times 10^{(32/n)-17}$ centimeters. The space spanned by the new dimensions is called "the bulk." In this theory, the particles of the standard model live within our familiar realm of three spatial dimensions, which forms a three-dimensional (hypersurface) membrane or "3-brane" within the bulk. The propagation of electroweak and strong nuclear forces is then confined to our 3-brane. However, at distances (r) less than R, gravity (via gravitons) propagates in the full $(3 + n)$-dimensional space, whereby its strength falls as $r^{-(2+n)}$ with increasing separation r. When $r > R$, the gravitational force reverts to its normal Newtonian r^{-2} falloff because there is no longer any extra-dimensional space for it to spread into. If $n = 1$, then the size of the extra-dimension would have to be $R \approx 2 \times 10^{15}$ cm (or 2×10^{10} km = 133.3 AU; 1 AU = 1.5×10^8 km is the mean Earth-Sun distance) in order to account for the weakness of gravity, but an extra space dimension this large would have already made itself obvious in the observed dynamics of the solar system. For this reason, investigators have discounted the possibility that $n = 1$. If $n = 2$, then the size of both extra space dimensions would have to be $R \approx 0.2$ cm (or 2 mm). In any case, inconspicuous neighboring 3-branes may be separated from the 3-brane we live on by only a fraction of a millimeter, or even much smaller distances, across the higher-dimensional bulk. Such neighboring 3-branes may be distant folds of our own 3-brane, with the same physics, but able to influence us across shortcuts through the bulk. Or they may be completely separate 3-branes possessing their own fundamental laws and parameters of nature that are completely different from our own. Several tabletop Cavendish-type experiments are now looking for sub-millimeter deviations from Newtonian gravitation as a first step towards verifying 3-brane theory, and other experiments are now being planned or are already underway (Pease, 2001). At present the preliminary experimental results have been negative for the existence of extra space dimensions, and the experimental data suggests that two extra space dimensions are now constrained to length scales << 0.2 – 0.3 millimeters while seven extra space dimensions can be no larger than 2 femtometers (Pease, 2001).

➤ Parallel Universes/Parallel Spaces (Everett, 1957; Wheeler, 1957, 1962; DeWitt, 1970; DeWitt and Graham, 1973; Jammer, 1974; Davies, 1980; Wolf, 1988; Kaku, 1994; Visser, 1995 and Section 2.1): There are only two other research tracts that are concerned with parallel universes besides 3-brane theory. The first tract is the traversable wormhole research that was discussed in Section 2.1. Traversable wormholes can connect many different universes in the "multiverse" (i.e., a conglomeration of many universes), and these are called inter-universe wormholes. However, traversable wormhole physics (a.k.a. Einstein's General Relativity Theory) does not provide a physical prescription for the existence and nature (i.e., fundamental parameters and physical laws) of other putative universes. The difference between inter-universe and intra-universe (i.e., two distant regions of one universe are connected with each other) wormholes arises only at the level of global geometry and global topology. Local physics near the throat of a traversable wormhole is insensitive to issues of intra-universal or inter-universal travel. An observer in the vicinity of the throat, while making local measurements, would not be able to tell whether he was traveling to another universe or to a remote part of our own universe. And one cannot rely on the topological (as opposed to geometrical) information to determine which is the case, because topological information is not enough to uniquely characterize an inter-universe connection. And General Relativity Theory does not fix the topology of spacetime, so we cannot ascertain the existence of other universes. [Note: Traversable wormholes are also geometrically possible for higher dimensional spaces.] The second tract is the "Many Worlds" interpretation of quantum theory. This version of quantum theory requires the simultaneous existence of an infinite number of equally real worlds, all of which are more-or-less causally disjoint, in order to interpret consistently the relationship between observed phenomena and observers. The theory was proposed in an attempt to overcome a number of deep paradoxes inherent in the interpretation of the theory of measurement and quantum theory. The Many Worlds theory argues that quantum theory requires the existence of a "superspace" of worlds spanning the range of all possible quantum observations (or quantum measurements). Through our acts of measurement we are imagined to trace a path through the mesh of possible outcomes. All the "worlds" are causally disjoint, and the uncertainty of quantum observation can be interpreted as an artifact of our access to such a limited portion of the superspace of possible worlds. The evolution in the superspace as a whole is entirely deterministic.

At present, <u>none</u> of the theoretical concepts outlined above have been brought to a level of technical maturity, where it becomes meaningful to ascertain whether any form of e-Teleportation is theoretically possible between extra space dimensions and different or parallel universes/spaces. However, as mentioned in the item on parallel universes/parallel spaces, there is the exception that traversable wormholes (three- and higher-dimensional) provide a solid physics principle for the implementation of teleportation between parallel universes/spaces. And traversable wormholes can be devised to connect 3-branes together. See Section 2.1 for the discussion on teleportation via traversable wormholes. Also, Kaluza-Klein theories, superstring theories and D-brane theory all have the common feature that their extra space dimensions are $\leq 10^{-35}$ m in extent, which makes it impossible for any useful form of macroscopic-level teleportation to occur between space dimensions. Last, it is not yet possible to do theoretical calculations or even experimentally verify most of these theories. Three-brane theory is the best parallel space theory there is, with the possibility that macroscopic-level teleportation is possible between space dimensions (only if the extra space dimension(s) has length scale(s) $>>$ millimeters). But this theory is still in the stage of maturing theoretically and achieving experimental verification (or falsification). Therefore, we can go no further in this section.

4.2 Vacuum Hole Teleportation

An unusual teleportation concept has been proposed by Leshan (1999, 2002), which describes the teleportation of objects throughout our universe by using the geometrical properties of spacetime. The proposal posits that there is a "zero-space" that exists outside the boundary of our universe, whereby this zero-space is a "point form" space, where the distance between any two points is always equal to zero. Leshan also calls this space a "hole." Further requirements and assumptions of the model are:

❏ time does not exist as a property in zero-space

❏ the cosmological principle (i.e., there are no privileged frames relative to another place or point in the universe) requires that the boundary or border of the universe must pass through every point of space

❏ virtual holes (or zero-space) in spacetime must exist at every point of the universe, which are also called "vacuum holes"

❏ vacuum holes exist as virtual particles

The last item is interesting because it implicitly says that vacuum holes (a.k.a. zero-space) must also be virtual particles, and in Section 2.2 we showed that virtual particles are a representation of the vacuum ZPF. Therefore, this infers that vacuum holes can be considered to be vacuum zero-point fluctuations in

TELEPORTATION

Leshan's model. Thus, a teleportation mechanism can arise in this model because distances between zero-space and any other point in the universe are zero, so that the vacuum holes can potentially exist at every point in the universe simultaneously. Therefore, if an object is sent "out of the universe" and into a vacuum hole (a.k.a. zero-space), then the object can appear at random at any spacetime point in the universe.

The mechanism for teleportation in this model is:

➢ to send an object outside of the universe by creating a closed surface (i.e., "hole sphere"), which consists of vacuum holes, around the object;

➢ while inside the hole sphere, the object then ceases to exist because objects cannot really exist outside of the universe;

➢ however, the object simultaneously exists at any other remote location in the universe (via the cosmological principle) at the instant it became enclosed by the hole sphere;

➢ therefore, it has been teleported to some remote location in the universe

Leshan points out that the teleportation device must curve spacetime so that the starting and destination points in the universe coincide, and the curved geometry must be similar to that of a black hole for an instant, so that a channel between the two points can be formed. (This sounds suspiciously like creating a traversable wormhole via an Einstein-Rosen bridge, which can be made traversable by perturbing the Schwarzschild spacetime metric an infinitesimal amount.) There is no space to traverse, so therefore there will be no passage of time during teleportation. The only expenditure of energy in this teleportation scheme is the energy that will be needed to curve spacetime.

This teleportation concept is very convoluted. Leshan does not offer any further explanations that are useful nor does he offer any precise technical description for the vacuum holes, and how they are to be produced and manipulated. There is also no mathematical physics derivation published by Leshan to support this concept. I am totally unable to evaluate this concept in the absence of a rigorous theoretical framework. This concept is too sketchy and full of technical "holes" to seriously consider it any further for this study. The reader should note that it has already been demonstrated that traversable wormholes are the best physical principle available to implement teleportation between universes and extra space dimensions.

4.3 Conclusion and Recommendations

At present, none of the theoretical concepts explored in this chapter have been brought to a level of technical maturity, where it becomes meaningful to ascertain whether any form of e-Teleportation is theoretically possible between extra space dimensions and different or parallel universes/spaces. However, there is the exception that traversable wormholes (three- and higher-dimensional) provide a solid physics principle for the implementation of teleportation between parallel universes/spaces. And traversable wormholes can be devised to connect 3-branes together. Kaluza-Klein, superstring and D-brane theories do not allow for any useful form of macroscopic-level teleportation to occur between space dimensions, because these theories require that the extra space dimensions be $\leq 10^{-35}$ m in extent. Last, it is not yet possible to do theoretical calculations to make predictions or even to experimentally verify most of these theories. Three-brane theory is the best parallel space theory there is with the possibility that macroscopic-level teleportation is possible between space dimensions. But this theory is still in the stage of maturing theoretically and getting experimental verification.

TELEPORTATION

- **Recommendations**:

  ➢ The recommendations outlined in Section 2.3 are relevant to the investigation of the possibility for e-Teleportation.

TELEPORTATION

5.0 p-TELEPORTATION

5.1 PK Phenomenon

P-Teleportation is a form of psychokinesis (or PK) similar to telekinesis but generally used to designate the movement of objects (called apports) through other physical objects or over great distances. Telekinesis is a form of PK, which describes the movement of stationary objects without the use of any known physical force. And PK is essentially the direct influence of mind on matter without any known intermediate physical energy or instrumentation. Rigorously controlled modern scientific laboratory PK, and related psychic (a.k.a. "psi", "paranormal" or parapsychology), research has been performed and/or documented by Rhine (1970), Schmidt (1974), Mitchell (1974a, b, see also the references cited therein), Swann (1974), Puthoff and Targ (1974, 1975), Hasted et al. (1975), Targ and Puthoff (1977), Nash (1978, see also the references cited therein), Shigemi et al. (1978), Hasted (1979), Houck (1984a), Wolman et al. (1986, see also the references cited therein), Schmidt (1987), Alexander et al. (1990), Giroldini (1991), Gissurarson (1992), Radin (1997, see also the references cited therein), Tart et al. (2002), Shoup (2002), and Alexander (2003).

A well-known theoretical/experimental/operational program directed by H. E. Puthoff, R. Targ, E. May and I. Swann was conducted at SRI International and the NSA, and sponsored at various times by the Central Intelligence Agency (CIA), the Defense Intelligence Agency (DIA), and the Army Intelligence and Security Command (INSCOM) over more than two decades; and the program was later carried on by E. May at SAIC (Alexander, 1980; Puthoff, 1996; Targ, 1996; Schnabel, 1997; Tart et al., 2002). This was called the Remote Viewing program, and it was a compartmentalized special access program possessing a variety of codenames during its 22 years of operation. Remote viewing involves precognition and clairvoyance, and it allows a practitioner to acquire information irrespective of intervening distance or time. The Remote Viewing program ended in 1994 and President W. J. Clinton officially declassified it in 1995. The reader should note that the very first U. S. military-intelligence R&D programs on psi, PK and mind control were conducted by H. K. (Andrija) Puharich, M.D., L.L.D during his military service at the Army Chemical and Biological Warfare Center at Fort Detrick, Maryland in the 1940s-50s. Puharich had an interest in clairvoyance and PK, and dabbled in theories for electronically and pharmaceutically enhancing and synthesizing psychic abilities. While in the Army, Puharich took part in a variety of parapsychology experiments, and he lectured Army, Air Force and Navy groups on possibilities for mind warfare. He was a recognized expert in hypnotism and microelectronics.

PK phenomenon was also explored in the Remote Viewing program. Col. J. B. Alexander (USA ret.) credits professional aerospace engineer Jack Houck for "capturing PK phenomenon and transitioning it into an observable form" (Houck, 1982, 1984a, b; Alexander et al., 1990; Alexander, 2003). During the past three decades, Houck (along with Alexander) held a number of PK sessions, whereby attendees are taught the PK induction process, and initiate their own PK events using various metal specimens (forks, spoons, etc.). Individuals were able to completely bend or contort their metal specimens with no physical force being applied whatsoever. Numerous government science advisors and senior military officials took part in and/or witnessed these events, which took place at the Pentagon, at officers' or scientists' homes, and at one quarterly INSCOM retreat attended by the commanding general and a group of colonels and generals commanding INSCOM units around the globe. Spontaneous deformation of the metal specimens was observed at the PK session conducted during the INSCOM retreat, causing a great deal of excitement among those present. Other notable trained observers were also present at this session, and they critically reviewed the events. Psychic Uri Geller (1975) is the original model for demonstrating

TELEPORTATION

PK metal bending. During a talk that he gave at the U.S. Capitol building, Uri caused a spoon to curve upward with no force applied, and then the spoon continued to bend <u>after</u> he put it back down and continued with his talk (Alexander, 1996). Jack Houck continues doing extensive experimental work and data collection on micro- and macro-PK phenomena. Scientifically controlled PK experiments at the Princeton University Engineering Anomalies Research Laboratory were conducted by Robert Jahn (Dean Emeritus of the School of Engineering), who reported that repeatedly consistent results in <u>mentally affecting</u> material substances has been demonstrated in the lab (Jahn and Dunne, 1987). In the 1980s, Jahn attended a meeting on the PK topic at the Naval Research Laboratory, and warned that foreign adversaries could exploit micro- or macro-PK to induce U.S. military fighter pilots to lose control of their aircraft and crash.

Very early investigations of, and experiments on, p-Teleportation occurred during the 19th and early 20th centuries. Many cases that were studied, and the experiments that were performed, were undoubtedly due to fraud, and few experiments have occurred under controlled conditions during that period. However, most of the credible, scientific reports of p-Teleportation phenomenon and related (controlled) experiments occurred in the late 20th century (see for example, Alexander et al., 1990; Radin, 1997). Some of that scientific work involved the investigation of Uri Geller and a variety of other recurrent spontaneous PK phenomena (Hasted et al., 1975; Puthoff and Targ, 1975; Targ and Puthoff, 1977; Nash, 1978; Wolman et al., 1986). Psychics Uri Geller (1975) and Ray Stanford (1974) claimed to have been teleported on several occasions. Most claimed instances of human teleportation of the body from one place to another have been unwitnessed. There are also a small number of credible reports of individuals who reported being teleported to/from UFOs during a UFO close encounter, which were scientifically investigated (Vallee, 1988, 1990, 1997). But there are a larger number of such reports that are anecdotal, whereby the witness data tends to be unreliable. However, we will confine our discussion to the controlled laboratory experiments that have been performed and reported.

One of the more interesting examples of controlled experiments with Uri Geller was one in which he was able to cause a part of a vanadium carbide crystal to vanish (Hasted et al., 1975). The crystal was encapsulated so it could not be touched, and it was placed in such a way that it could not be switched with another crystal by sleight of hand. A more spectacular series of rigorously controlled (and repeatable!) laboratory experiments occurred in the Peoples Republic of China (PRC). In September 1981, an extraordinary paper was published in the PRC in the journal Ziran Zazhi (transl.: Nature Journal), and this paper was entitled, "Some Experiments on the Transfer of Objects Performed by Unusual Abilities of the Human Body" (Shuhuang et al., 1981). The paper reported that gifted children were able to cause the apparent teleportation of small objects (radio micro-transmitters, photosensitive paper, mechanical watches, horseflies, other insects, etc.) from one location to another (that was meters away) without them ever touching the objects beforehand. The experiments were operated under exceptionally well-controlled conditions (both blind and double-blind). The researchers involved included not only observers from various PRC colleges and medical research institutes, but also representatives from the PRC National Defense Science Commission. Because of the involvement of the latter, it was deemed necessary that an unclassified Intelligence Information Report be prepared by the DIA (see Shuhuang et al., 1981), which included a detailed English translation of the article.

Additional research carried out by the Aerospace Medicine Engineering Institute in Beijing was reported in the July 1990 issue of the Chinese Journal of Somatic Science (Kongzhi et al., 1990; Jinggen et al., 1990; Banghui, 1990), which was also translated into English by the DIA. Reported in several articles are experiments involving the videotaping and high-speed photography of the transfer of test specimens (nuts, bundles of matches, pills, nails, thread, photosensitive paper, chemically treated paper, sponges dipped in $FeCl_3$, etc.) through the walls of sealed paper envelopes, double layered KCNS type paper bags, sealed glass bottles and tubes with sealed caps, and sealed plastic film canisters without the walls of any of these containers being breached. All of the Chinese experiments reported using gifted children and young adults, who possessed well-known extraordinary PK ability, to cause the teleportation of the various test specimens. In all the experimental cases that were reported, the test specimens that were teleported were completely unaltered or unchanged from their initial state, even the insects were

TELEPORTATION

unaffected by being teleported. The experiments were well controlled, scientifically recorded, and the experimental results were always repeatable.

The Chinese papers are all extremely interesting and very well written, and they show photographs and schematic diagrams of the various experimental setups. The experimental protocols were explained in lengthy detail, and thorough data and statistical analysis were presented in the results. The combined results from the several Chinese experiments showed that:

➢ different research groups designed different experimental protocols, used different gifted psychics, used different sealed containers, and used different test specimens (live insects, bulk inanimate objects, and even radio micro-transmitters were used to track the location of the specimens) that were to be teleported;

➢ the time required for the teleportation of test specimens through various barriers was anywhere from a fraction of a second to several minutes, and this was not dependent on the test specimen that was used, the sealed container that was used (or its barrier thickness), which experimental protocol was used, or which psychic was being used

➢ the high-speed photography/videotaping recorded in one series of experiments that test specimens would physically "meld" or blend with the walls of sealed containers; and recorded in a different series of experiments that test specimens would simply disappear from inside the container only to reappear at another location (after seconds to several minutes of time transpired), such that the test specimen did not actually undergo total material disintegration/reintegration during teleportation – this data is important, because without the aid of electronic monitoring instruments, the average person's sensory organs and usual methods of detection are temporarily unable to perceive the test specimen's (ambiguous) existence during the teleportation process;

➢ the radio micro-transmitter used as a test specimen in one series of experiments (Shuhuang et al., 1981) transmitted a radio signal to several stationary electronic instruments/receivers, so that the specimen could be tracked and monitored (via signal amplitude and frequency measurements) during the teleportation process; the experimenters discovered that there was large fluctuations in the intensity (in both amplitude and frequency) of the monitored signal to the effect that it would either completely disappear or become extremely weak (to the extent that the monitoring instruments could scarcely detect it) – it was discovered that there was a definite correlation between the change in strength (i.e., radical frequency shifts were observed) of the monitored radio signal and the teleportation of the test specimen, such that the weak or absent signal indicated that the specimen was "nonexistent" (or in an altered physical state) during teleportation (note: the monitored signal amplitude and frequency of the micro-transmitter specimen were stable before and after teleportation);

➢ before and after "passing through the container wall/barrier", the test specimen and the container's wall/barrier are both complete solid objects;

➢ the gifted psychics were never allowed to see (they were blindfolded in many experiments) or touch each of the test specimens or the sealed containers before and after experiments were conducted, and only the experimenters touched the specimens and containers (using both blind and double-blind protocols);

➢ the experimental results were all repeatable

TELEPORTATION

➢ the conditions for fraud and sleight of hand were totally eliminated, and multiple independent outside witnesses (technical and military-intelligence experts) were present at all times to ensure total fidelity of the experiments

The experimental radio micro-transmitter and high-speed photography/videotaping data offer an important clue on what the teleportation mechanism is, and this will be discussed further in Section 5.1.1. The Chinese were unable to offer any significant physics hypothesis that could explain their results. Some researchers stated that it is necessary to invoke a new physics, which somehow unifies the human consciousness (i.e., physics of consciousness) with quantum and spacetime physics, in order to understand p-Teleportation and related PK phenomena. The researchers were amazed by their repeated results, and were barely able to fathom the altered "state of being" that test specimens underwent during teleportation.

It is also important to point out that during the Cold War the DIA produced three (now declassified) reports on the parapsychology research of the Soviet Union and its Warsaw Pack allies (LaMothe, 1972; Maire and LaMothe, 1975; DIA Report, 1978; other related studies were reported by Groller, 1986, 1987). The purpose of the reports was to collate and summarize collected intelligence, describe in great detail, and assess the Soviet Union and Warsaw Pact R&D on parapsychology and paraphysics. The reports outlined the history of pre-revolutionary (Czarist) Russian, and WWII and post-WWII era Soviet R&D on psychotronics, human mind/behavior control, and the entire spectrum of parapsychology. The Soviet information also mentions the psychotronic/parapsychology R&D materials that Soviet military forces took from various Nazi research centers in and around Germany at the end of WWII. The entire spectrum of parapsychology phenomena was explored by the Soviets, which resulted in the generation of a wealth of experimental data and related scientific research literature. One DIA report noted that there was an East versus West science debate in the Soviet literature over whether paranormal phenomenon and related experimental data was real or even scientifically sound in comparison to western scientific practice and philosophy. Another DIA report lists the names and affiliations of all the researchers, as well as the names of the various Soviet and Warsaw Pact research centers, that were involved. Also, Pratt (1986) reviews and summarizes the history of Soviet psychotronics research.

The U.S. military-intelligence establishment was concerned with the possibility that the Soviets and their Warsaw Pact allies were conducting psychotronics and mind control R&D in order to discover how to exploit and control powerful phenomena that could be used against the U.S. and its allies. LaMothe (1972) chronicled how the Soviets had been researching methods of influencing human behavior for over sixty years. The Soviets and their allies extensively explored an influence technology that they called "controlled offensive behavior", which is defined as "research on human vulnerability as it applies to methods of influencing or altering human behavior" (LaMothe, 1972). Also, LaMothe (1972) describes the revolutionary techniques the Soviets studied to influence human behavior, which included: sound, light, color, odors, sensory deprivation, sleep, electromagnetic fields, biochemicals, autosuggestion, hypnosis, and parapsychology phenomena (such as psychokinesis, telekinesis, extrasensory perception-ESP, astral projection, clairvoyance, precognition, and dream state, etc.). The LaMothe (1972) report became an aid in the development of countermeasures for the protection of U.S. and/or allied personnel.

Psychotronics is the general term that was used in the former Soviet Union/Warsaw Pact countries to categorize many psychic phenomena undergoing scientific research. The conclusions that were reached in the DIA reports are that within the category of psychotronics, the Soviets identified two discrete skills (LaMothe, 1972):

➢ bioenergetics: those phenomena associated with the production of objectively detectable effects such as psychokinesis, telekinesis, levitation effects, transformations of energy, i.e. the altering or affecting of matter

➢ bioinformation: those phenomena associated with the obtaining of information through means other than the normal sensory channels (i.e., ESP), such as telepathy, precognition, and

TELEPORTATION

clairvoyance, i.e., using the mind to tap into the thoughts of others or to acquire present or future information about objective events in the world

These phenomena involve using the mind and/or some "field" of the body to affect other minds and inanimate objects irrespective of intervening distance or elapsed time, and without engaging any conventional tools. Bioenergetics and bioinformation are two classifications that form a single branch of science the Soviets preferred to call biocommunications. Soviet biocommunications research is primarily concerned with exploring the existence of a definite group of natural phenomena controlled by laws that are not based on any known (energetic) influence. The types of biocommunication (a.k.a. psychotronics) phenomena includes special sensory biophysical activities, brain and mind control, telepathic communications or bioinformation transceiving, bioluminescent and bioenergetic emissions, and the effects of altered states of consciousness on the human psyche. Psychotronics and remote viewing provide capabilities that have obvious intelligence applications. The Soviets and their Warsaw Pact allies invested millions of dollars in psychotronics R&D because they understood this, and saw the potential payoff for military and intelligence applications.

The U.S. response to Soviet psychotronics R&D programs was the Remote Viewing program. In addition, the U.S. Army began the JEDI Project in 1983, which sought to increase human potential using teachable models of behavioral/physical excellent by unconventional means (Alexander et al., 1990). The JEDI Project was essentially a human-performance modeling experiment based on neuro-linguistic programming (NLP) skills, whereby advanced influence technologies to model excellence in human performance was used. The program ran under the auspices of the Army INSCOM and the Organizational Effectiveness School, and was sponsored by a U.S. government interagency task force. Finally, it should be pointed out that the program had successfully trained several hundred people, including members of Congress (such as Al Gore, Jr. and Tom Downey), before being terminated.

There is a wealth of factual scientific research data from around the world attesting to the physical reality of p-Teleportation and related anomalous psi phenomena (Mitchell, 1974b; Targ and Puthoff, 1977; Nash, 1978; Radin, 1997; Tart et al., 2002). The skeptical reader should not be so quick to dismiss the subject matter in this chapter, because one must remain open-minded about this subject and consider p-Teleportation as worthy of further scientific exploration. The psychotronics topic is controversial within the western scientific community. The debate among scientists and scientific philosophers is highly charged at times, and becomes acrimonious to the point where reputable skeptical scientists cease being impartial by refusing to examine the experimental data or theories, and they prefer to bypass rational discourse by engaging in ad hominem attacks and irrational "armchair" arguments.

P-Teleportation and related phenomena are truly anomalous, and they challenge accepted modern scientific paradigm. Lightman and Gingerich (1991) wrote, "Scientists are reluctant to change paradigms for the purely psychological reasons that the familiar is often more comfortable than the unfamiliar and that inconsistencies in belief are uncomfortable." And theories change over time when anomalies enter the picture. Anomalies are particularly helpful for they point to the inadequacies of an old model and point the way to a new one. Anomalous scientific facts are unexpected and difficult to explain within an existing conceptual framework. Kuhn (1970) describes scientific discovery as a complex process, in which an anomalous fact of nature is recognized, and then followed by a change in conceptual framework (i.e., paradigm) that makes the new fact no longer an anomaly. Kuhn stated that, "Discovery commences with the awareness of anomaly, that is, with the recognition that nature has somehow violated the pre-induced expectations that govern normal science." This statement neatly describes exactly what transpired during the historical revolution that took place in physics between the classical mechanics/electrodynamics age in the 19th century and the quantum/atomic/nuclear/relativistic age in the 20th century. And this isn't the only time in human history that scientific paradigms have dramatically changed. The discovery of p-Teleportation already commenced in the 20th century, so let us continue the discovery and create a new physics paradigm for the 21st century.

TELEPORTATION

5.1.1 Hypothesis Based on Mathematical Geometry

The Chinese researchers reported in their teleportation experiments that high-speed photography/videotaping recorded test specimens physically "melding" or blending with the walls of sealed containers, and in a different series of experiments the test specimens would simply disappear from inside the container only to reappear at another location (after seconds to several minutes of time transpired). They also reported in the series of radio micro-transmitter experiments that there were large fluctuations in the intensity (in both amplitude and frequency) of the monitored signal to the effect that it would either completely disappear or become extremely weak (to the extent that the monitoring instruments could scarcely detect it); and they discovered that there was a definite correlation between the change in strength (i.e., radical frequency shifts were observed) of the monitored radio signal and the teleportation of the radio micro-transmitter, such that the weak or absent signal indicated that the specimen was "nonexistent" (or in an altered physical state) during teleportation. This data is important because without the aid of electronic monitoring instruments, the average person's sensory organs and usual methods of detection are temporarily unable to perceive the test specimen's (ambiguous) existence during the teleportation process. This data offers an important clue on what the teleportation mechanism is.

It is beyond the scope of this study to propose a complete self-consistent physics theory of consciousness/mind, which explains how the mind can activate p-Teleportation and related psychotronics phenomena. This topic has been under study in recent decades by a legion of medical science, bio- and neuro-physiology, psychology, mathematics, philosophy, and physics experts. Many different theories with varying degree of theoretical maturity and self-consistency have been proposed over the years, and most of them have not yet been experimentally tested for various reasons. However, some first-order experimental work has been done (Mitchell, 1974b; Targ and Puthoff, 1977; Wolman et al., 1986; Radin, 1997; Tart et al., 2002). Ironically, quantum mechanics theory, and the related physics of quantum entanglement and teleportation, has become the primary focus of all of the physics theories of consciousness/psychotronics that have been recently proposed (see for example, Shan, 2003). Wolman et al. (1986) and Radin (1997) provide a review and discussion on recent theories and experiments that are based on quantum physics theory (see also, Walker, 1974; Targ and Puthoff, 1977; Mitchell, 1999, and the references cited therein; Tart et al., 2002). It appears that the physics of q-Teleportation (Chapter 3) has tremendous relevance to the physics of p-Teleportation and psychotronics.

In the following I propose a parsimonious first-order hypothesis that can explain the gross features of both the Chinese p-Teleportation data and the other reported p-Teleportation phenomena. But I will refrain from including any role that might be played by quantum phenomena since the scientific community has not yet settled that particular issue. (However, it is apparent that quantum theory and quantum phenomena will likely play a key role in a formal physics theory of PK and psychotronics.)

First-Order Hypothesis:

❑ Fact 1: The mature discipline of mathematical geometry developed the properties of higher dimensional spaces (Reichenbach, 1957; Manning, 1977; Rucker, 1977). An example of one such property that is of relevance to the hypothesis: One can visualize a four-dimensional world by using color as the 4th dimension. We can think of a three-dimensional world, whereby objects pass through one another if their colors (i.e., four-dimensional locations) are different (Reichenbach, 1957). For example, color can be used as a 4th dimension to see how a knot in three-dimensions can be untied in a 4th spatial dimension without moving the ends of the cord. That is because a cord cannot stay knotted in four-dimensional space, because the extra degree of freedom will cause any knot to slip through itself. Two other interesting and relevant examples are that the links of a chain may be separated unbroken in the 4th dimension, and a flexible sphere may be turned inside out without tearing in the 4th dimension (Manning, 1977; Rucker, 1977).

TELEPORTATION

❑ Proposition 1 and Fact 2: It has been proposed that our space actually possesses a slight four-dimensional hyperthickness, so that the ultimate components of our nervous system are actually higher dimensional, thus enabling the human mind/brain to imagine four-dimensional space (Hinton, 1888, 1904; Rucker, 1977). If this is the case, then the three-dimensional nets of neurons that code thoughts in our brain may form four-dimensional patterns to achieve four-dimensional thought. The "bulk" space in 3-brane theory (see Section 4.1), and experimental data from the Remote Viewing program (see Section 5.1), provide support for this concept. Can we see into the 4th dimension and have four-dimensional thoughts? Yes, we can. Proof (see, Rucker, 1977, 1984): If you look at a Necker cube for a while, it spontaneously turns into its mirror image and back again. If you watch it do this often enough, the twinkling sort of motion from one state to the other begins to seem like a continuous motion. But this motion can only be continuous if it is a rotation in four-dimensional space. The mathematician August F. Möbius discovered in 1827 that it is in fact possible to turn a three-dimensional solid object into its mirror image by an appropriate rotation through four-dimensional space (a.k.a. hyperspace rotation). Thus, it is actually possible for our minds to perform such a rotation. Therefore, we can actually produce four-dimensional phenomenon in our minds, so our consciousness is four-dimensional. Rucker (1984) shows another dramatic example of being able to see into the 4th dimension via a "Neck-A-Cube."

❑ Fact 3: Another property of higher dimensional geometry (Reichenbach, 1957; Rucker, 1977, 1984) is that one can move through solid three-dimensional obstacles without penetrating them by passing in the direction of the 4th (spatial) dimension. The 4th dimension is perpendicular to all of our normal three-dimensional space directions, and so our three-dimensional enclosures have no walls against this direction.

❑ Conclusion and Hypothesis: Therefore, the results of the Chinese p-Teleportation experiments can simply be explained as a human consciousness phenomenon that somehow acts to move or rotate test specimens through a 4th spatial dimension, so that the specimens are able to penetrate the solid walls/barriers of their containers without physically breaching them. No real dematerialization/rematerialization of the specimens takes place. The intensity fluctuations of the radio micro-transmitter specimen's electromagnetic signal, and the apparent blending of the other specimens with the walls of their containers, represent the passage of the specimens through a 4th spatial dimension. During teleportation the radio signals emitted by the micro-transmitter became weak/non-existent and fluctuated, because they were spreading out into the 4th dimension and became undetectable in our three-dimensional space. The weak signals that were ("barely") detected represent the leakage of a portion of the radio signal back into our three-dimensional space from the 4th dimension during teleportation. The observed blending of the other specimens with the walls of their containers is how the movement/rotation of the specimens through the 4th dimension was visually interpreted by the mind (along the lines of the Necker cube or Neck-A-Cube examples).

5.2 Conclusion and Recommendations

We will need a physics theory of consciousness and psychotronics, along with more experimental data, in order to test the hypothesis in Section 5.1.1 and discover the physical mechanisms that lay behind the psychotronic manipulation of matter. P-Teleportation, if verified, would represent a phenomenon that could offer potential high-payoff military, intelligence and commercial applications. This phenomenon could generate a dramatic revolution in technology, which would result from a dramatic paradigm shift in science. Anomalies are the key to all paradigm shifts!

TELEPORTATION

•**Recommendations**:

➢ There are numerous supporters within the U.S. military establishment who comprehend the significance of remote viewing and PK phenomenon, and believe that they could have strategic implications. Bremseth (2001), a U.S. Navy SEAL, attended the Marine War College and studied the Remote Viewing program, and interviewed many of the former program participants. Bremseth then wrote his thesis on the topic, and concluded that the evidence supported continued research and applications of remote viewing. A research program improving on and expanding, or implementing novel variations of, the Chinese and Uri Geller-type experiments should be conducted in order to generate p-Teleportation phenomenon in the lab. The performances and characteristics of p-Teleportation need to be delineated in order to develop a refined hypothesis. Such a program should be designed so that an operational model for p-Teleportation can be developed and implemented as a prototype. An experimental program similar in fashion to the Remote Viewing program should be funded at $900,000 – 1,000,000 per year in parallel with a theoretical program funded at $500,000 per year for an initial five-year duration. The role of quantum physics theory and related quantum phenomena (i.e., entanglement and teleportation) in p-Teleportation and psychotronics should be explored in this program (see for example, the Biological Quantum Teleportation recommendation in Section 3.3). An experiment definition study should be conducted first to identify and propose the best experiments for this program, which should be funded at $80,000 for one year.

TELEPORTATION

6.0 REFERENCES

1. Aczel, A. D. (2002), <u>Entanglement: The Greatest Mystery in Physics</u>, Four Walls Eight Windows Press, New York

2. Aharonov, Y., Reznik, B. and Stern, A. (1998), "Quantum limitations of superluminal propagation," Phys. Rev. Lett., <u>81</u>, 2190-2193

3. Aharonov, Y. and Albert, D. (1981), "Can we make sense of the measurement process in relativistic quantum mechanics?," Phys. Rev. D, <u>24</u>, 359-370

4. Alexander, Col. J. B. (2003), <u>Winning The War: Advanced Weapons, Strategies, And Concepts For The Post-9/11 World</u>, St. Martin's Press, New York, pp. 238 – 244

5. Alexander, J. B. (1996), "Uri's Impact on the U.S. Army," posted on http://www.urigeller.com

6. Alexander, Lt. Col. J. B. (1980), "The New Mental Battlefield: 'Beam Me Up, Spock,'" Military Review, <u>vol. XL</u>, no. 12

7. Alexander, Col. J. B., Groller, Maj. R. and Morris, J. (1990), <u>The Warrior's Edge</u>, W. Morrow Co., New York

8. Ambjørn, J. and Wolfram, S. (1983), "Properties of the Vacuum. I. Mechanical and Thermodynamic," Annals Phys., <u>147</u>, 1-32

9. Antoniadis, I., Arkani-Hamed, N., Dimopoulos, S. and Dvali, G. (1998), "New dimensions at a millimeter to a fermi and superstrings at a TeV," Phys. Lett. B, <u>436</u>, 257-263

10. Appelquist, T., Chodos, A. and Freund, P. G. O. eds. (1987), <u>Modern Kaluza-Klein Theories</u>, Addison-Wesley, Menlo Park

11. Arkani-Hamed, N., Dimopoulos, S. and Dvali, G. (2002), "Large Extra Dimensions: A New Arena for Particle Physics," Physics Today, <u>55</u>, 35-40

12. Arkani-Hamed, N., Dimopoulos, S. and Dvali, G. (1998), "The hierarchy problem and new dimensions at a millimeter," Phys. Lett. B, <u>429</u>, 263-272

13. Arkani-Hamed, N., Dimopoulos, S., Kaloper, N. and Dvali, G. (2000), "Manyfold universe," Journal of High Energy Physics (JHEP online physics papers), http://jhep.sissa.it/archive/papers/jhep122000010/jhep122000010.pdf0012

14. Aspect, A. (1983), <u>Trois tests expérimentaux des inégalités de Bell par mesure de corrélation de polarisation de photons</u>, Ph.D. thesis No. 2674, Université de Paris-Sud, Centre D'Orsay

15. Aspect, A., Dalibard, J. and Roger, G. (1982a), "Experimental Tests of Bell's Inequalities Using Time-Varying Analyzers," Phys. Rev. Letters, <u>49</u>, 1804-1807

16. Aspect, A., Grangier, P. and Roger, G. (1982b), "Experimental Realization of Einstein-Podolsky-Rosen-Bohm Gedankenexperiment: A New Violation of Bell's Inequalities," Phys. Rev. Letters, <u>49</u>, 91

17. Aspect, A. and Grangier, P. (1985), Lettere al Nuovo Cimento, <u>43</u>, 345

18. Aspelmeyer, M., et al. (2003), "Long-Distance Free-Space Distribution of Quantum Entanglement," Science, <u>301</u>, 621 - 623

19. Banghui, W. (1990), "Evidence of the Existence of Abnormal States of Matter," Chinese J. Somatic Sci., <u>First Issue</u>, 36 [translated into English by the Defense Intelligence Agency]

20. Barcelo, C. and Visser, M. (2002), "Twilight for the energy conditions?," Int. J. Mod. Phys. D, <u>11</u>, 1553

21. Barnum, H., Caves, C., Fuchs, C., Jozsa, R. and Schumacher, B. (1996), "Noncommuting Mixed States Cannot Be Broadcast," Phys. Rev. Lett., <u>76</u>, 2818-2821

22. Bell, J. S. (1964), "On the Einstein Podolsky Rosen Paradox," Physics, <u>1</u>, 195

23. Bennett, C. H., et al. (1993), "Teleporting an unknown quantum state via dual classical and Einstein-Podolsky-Rosen channels," Phys. Rev. Lett., <u>70</u>, 1895-1899

24. Bennett, C. H. and Wiesner, S. J. (1992), "Communication via one- and two-particle operators on Einstein-Podolsky-Rosen states," Phys. Rev. Lett., <u>69</u>, 2881-2884

TELEPORTATION

25. Bennett, G. L., Forward, R. L. and Frisbee, R. H. (1995), "Report on the NASA/JPL Workshop on Advanced Quantum/Relativity Theory Propulsion," AIAA-95-2599, 31st AIAA/ASME/ASE/ASEE Joint Propulsion Conference and Exhibit, San Diego, CA

26. Birrell, N. D. and Davies, P. C. W. (1982), Quantum fields in curved space, Cambridge University Press, Cambridge

27. Blaauboer, M., et al. (1998), "Superluminal pulse transmission through a phase conjugating mirror," Optics Communications, 148, 295-299

28. Boschi, D., et al. (1998), "Experimental realization of teleporting an unknown pure quantum state via dual classical and Einstein-Podolski-Rosen channels," Phys. Rev. Lett., 80, 1121-1125

29. Bose, S. and Home, D. (2002), "Generic Entanglement Generation, Quantum Statistics, and Complementarity," Phys. Rev. Lett., 88, 050401

30. Bose, S., Knight, P. L., Plenio, M. B. and Vedral, V. (1999), "Proposal for Teleportation of an Atomic State via Cavity Decay," Phys. Rev. Lett., 83, 5158-5161

31. Bouwmeester, D., et al. (1997), "Experimental quantum teleportation," Nature, 390, 575-579

32. Bowen, W. P., et al. (2003), "Experimental investigation of continuous variable quantum teleportation," Phys. Rev. A, 67, 032302

33. Bowen, W. P., Treps, N., Schnabel, R. and Lam, P. K. (2002), "Experimental demonstration of continuous variable polarization entanglement," Phys. Rev. Lett., 89, 253601

34. Brassard, G., Braunstein, S. and Cleve, R. (1998), "Teleportation as a quantum computation," Physica D, 120, 43-47

35. Braunstein, S. (1996), "Quantum teleportation without irreversible detection," Proc. Royal Acad., 53, 1900-1903

36. Braunstein, S., Fuchs, C., Kimble, H. and van Loock, P. (2001), "Quantum versus classical domains for teleportation with continuous variables," Phys. Rev. A, 64, 022321

37. Braunstein, S. and Kimble, J. (1998), "Teleportation of continuous quantum variables," Phys. Rev. Lett., 80, 869-872

38. Bremseth, Cmdr. L. R. (2001), Unconventional Human Intelligence Support: Transcendent and Asymmetric Warfare Implications of Remote Viewing, Thesis, Marine War College

39. Buttler, W., et al. (1998), "Practical free-space quantum key distribution over 1 km," Phys. Rev. Lett., 81, 3283-3286

40. Center for Quantum Computation Web Site: http://www.qubit.org

41. Chan, H. B., et al. (2001), "Quantum Mechanical Actuation of Microelectromechanical Systems by the Casimir Force," Science, 291, 1941-1944

42. Chiao, R. and Steinberg, A. (1998), "Quantum optical studies of tunneling and other superluminal phenomena," Physica Scripta, T76, 61-66

43. Chown, M. (1990), "Can photons travel 'faster than light'?," New Scientist, 126, 32

44. CIA In-Q-Tel Web Site information: http://www.cia.gov/cia/publications/inqtel/

45. Cole, D. C. and Puthoff, H. E. (1993), "Extracting Energy and Heat from the Vacuum," Phys. Rev. E, 48, 1562

46. Davies, P. C. W. (1980), Other Worlds, Dent, London

47. Davis, E. W. (1999a), Research Summary Report #1 to Dr. Hal Puthoff, IASA: Brief Summary of "Lorentzian Wormholes From The Gravitationally Squeezed Vacuum", NASA Research Center Online Library – Interstellar Studies (available from the author)

48. Davis, E. W. (1999b), Research Summary Report #2 to Dr. Hal Puthoff, IASA: Brief Summary of "Gravitational Vacuum Polarization. Parts I – IV", NASA Research Center Online Library – Interstellar Studies (available from the author)

49. de Felice, F. (1971), "On the gravitational field acting as an optical medium," Gen. Rel. Grav., 2, 347-357

50. de Oliveira, E. C. and Rodriguez, W. (1998), "Superluminal electromagnetic waves in free space," Annalen der Physik, 7(7-8), 654-659

51. de Sabbata, V. and Schmutzer, E. eds. (1983), <u>Unified Field Theories of More Than 4 Dimensions, Proc. Int'l School of Cosmology and Gravitation (Erice)</u>, World Scientific, Singapore

52. Deutsch, D. (1998), <u>The Fabric of Reality</u>, Penguin Books

53. DeWitt, B. S. and Graham, N. eds. (1973), <u>The Many Worlds Interpretation of Quantum Mechanics</u>, Princeton University Press, Princeton

54. DeWitt, B. S. (1970), Physics Today, $\underline{23}$, 30

55. DIA Report (1978), <u>Paraphysics R&D – Warsaw Pact</u>, Defense Intelligence Agency, Report No. DST-1810S-202-78, DIA Task No. PT-1810-18-76, Washington DC (authors' names redacted)

56. Dicke, R. H. (1961), "Mach's principle and equivalence," in <u>Proc. of the Int'l School of Physics "Enrico Fermi" Course XX, Evidence for Gravitational Theories</u>, ed. C. Møller, Academic Press, New York, pp. 1-49

57. Dicke, R. H. (1957), "Gravitation without a principle of equivalence," Rev. Mod. Phys., $\underline{29}$, 363-376

58. Ding, Y. J. and Kaplan, A. E. (1992), "Nonlinear Magneto-Optical Effect in Vacuum: Inhomogeneity-Originated Second-Harmonic Generation in DC Magnetic Field," J. Nonl. Opt. Phys., $\underline{1}$, 51-72

59. Ding, Y. J. and Kaplan, A. E. (1989), "Nonlinear Magneto-Optics of Vacuum: Second-Harmonic Generation," Phys. Rev. Lett., $\underline{63}$, 2725-2728

60. Drummond, I. J. and Hathrell, S. J. (1980), "QED vacuum polarization in a background gravitational field and its effect on the velocity of photons," Phys. Rev. D, $\underline{22}$, 343-355

61. Dür, W. and Briegel, H.-J. (2003), "Entanglement purification for Quantum Computation," Phys. Rev. Lett., $\underline{90}$, 067901

62. Einstein, A., Podolsky, B. and Rosen, N. (1935), "Can quantum mechanical description of physical reality be considered complete?," Phys. Rev., $\underline{47}$, 777-780

63. Evans, J., Nandi, K. and Islam, A. (1996a), "The Optical-Mechanical Analogy in General Relativity: New Methods for the Paths of Light and of the Planets," Am. J. Phys., $\underline{64}$, 1401-1415

64. Evans, J., Nandi, K. and Islam, A. (1996b), "The Optical-Mechanical Analogy in General Relativity: Exact Newtonian Forms for the Equations of Motion of Particles and Photons," Gen. Rel. Grav., $\underline{28}$, 413-439

65. Everett, H. (1957), Rev. Mod. Phys., $\underline{29}$, 454

66. Forward, R. L. (2001), Personal Communication, Salt Lake City, UT

67. Forward, R. L. (1999), Personal Communication, Los Angeles, CA

68. Forward, R. L. (1998), "Apparent Method for Extraction of Propulsion Energy from the Vacuum," AIAA-98-3140, 34th AIAA/ASME/SAE/ASEE Joint Propulsion Conference & Exhibit, Cleveland, OH

69. Forward, R. L. (1996), <u>Mass Modification Experiment Definition Study</u>, PL-TR-96-3004, Phillips Laboratory-Propulsion Directorate, Air Force Materiel Command, Edwards AFB, CA

70. Forward, R. L. (1984), "Extracting electrical energy from the vacuum by cohesion of charged foliated conductors," Phys. Rev. B, $\underline{30}$, 1770-1773

71. Freedman, S. J. and Clauser, J. F. (1972), "Experimental Test of Local Hidden-Variable Theories," Phys. Rev. Lett., $\underline{28}$, 938-941

72. Friedman, J. et al. (1990), "Cauchy problem in spacetimes with closed timelike curves," Phys. Rev. D, $\underline{42}$, 1915-1930

73. Furusawa, A., et al. (1998), "Unconditional quantum teleportation," Science, $\underline{282}$, 706-710

74. Furuya, K., et al. (1999), "Failure of a proposed superluminal scheme," Phys. Lett. A, $\underline{251}$, 294-296

75. Geller, U. (1975), <u>Uri Geller: My Story</u>, Praeger Publ., New York

76. Giroldini, W. (1991), "Eccles's Model of Mind-Brain Interaction and Psychokinesis: A Preliminary Study," J. Sci. Explor., $\underline{5}$, no. 2

77. Gisin, N. (1990), "Weinberg's non-linear quantum mechanics and superluminal communications," Phys. Lett. A, 143, 1-2

78. Gisin, N., Scarani, V., Tittel, W. and Zbinden, H. (2000), "Optical tests of quantum non-locality: from EPR-Bell tests towards experiments with moving observers," Ann. Phys. (Leipzig), 9, 831-841

79. Gissurarson, L. R. (1992), "The Psychokinesis Effect: Geomagnetic Influence, Age and Sex Difference," J. Sci. Explor., 6, no. 2

80. Green, M. B. (1985), "Unification of forces and particles in superstring theories," Nature, 314, 409

81. Greenberger, D. (1998), "If one could build a macroscopical Schrodinger cat state, one could communicate superluminally," Physica Scripta, T76, 57-60

82. Groller, Capt. R. (1987), "Soviet Psychotronics – a Closer Look," Military Intelligence, PB 34-87-1 (Test), pp. 43-44

83. Groller, Capt. R. (1986), "Soviet Psychotronics – a State of Mind," Military Intelligence, 12, no. 4, pp. 18-21, 58

84. Hagley, E., et al. (1997), "Generation of Einstein-Podolsky-Rosen Pairs of Atoms," Phys. Rev. Lett., 79, 1-5

85. Hald, J., Sørensen, J. L., Schori, C. and Polzik, E. S. (1999), "Spin Squeezed Atoms: A Macroscopic Entangled Ensemble Created by Light," Phys. Rev. Lett., 83, 1319-1322

86. Hartle, J. B. and Hawking, S. W. (1983), "Wave function of the Universe," Phys. Rev. D, 28, 2960-2975

87. Hasted, J. B. (1979), "Paranormal Metal Bending," in The Iceland Papers: Selected Papers on Experimental and Theoretical Research on the Physics of Consciousness, Puharich, A. ed., Research Associates Publ., Amherst, WI

88. Hasted, J. B., Bohm, D., Bastin, E. W. and O'Reagan, B. (1975), "Scientists confronting the paranormal," Nature, 254, 470-472

89. Haugan, M. P. and Will, C. M. (1977), "Principles of equivalence, Eötvös experiments, and gravitational red-shift experiments: The free fall of electromagnetic systems to post—post-Coulombian order," Phys. Rev. D, 15, 2711-2720

90. Hawking, S. W. and Ellis, G. F. R. (1973), The Large-Scale Structure of Space-Time, Cambridge Univ. Press, Cambridge, pp. 88-91 and 95-96

91. Hegerfeldt, G. (1998), "Instantaneous spreading and Einstein causality in quantum theory," Annalen der Physik, 7(7-8), 716-725

92. Heitler, W. (1954), The Quantum Theory of Radiation (3rd ed.), Oxford University Press, London, p. 113.

93. Herrmann, F. (1989), "Energy Density and Stress: A New Approach to Teaching Electromagnetism", Am. J. Phys., 57, 707-714

94. Hinton, C. H. (1904), The Fourth Dimension, Sonnenschein, London

95. Hinton, C. H. (1888), A New Era of Thought, Sonnenschein, London

96. Hochberg, D. and Kephart, T. W. (1991), "Lorentzian wormholes from the gravitationally squeezed vacuum," Phys. Lett. B, 268, 377-383

97. Hong, C. K. and Mandel, L. (1985), "Theory of parametric frequency down conversion of light," Phys. Rev. A, 31, 2409-2418

98. Houck, J. (1984a), "Surface Change During Warm-Forming," Archaeus, 2, no. 1

99. Houck, J. (1984b), "PK Party History," Psi Research, 3, no. 1

100. Houck, J. (1982), "PK Party Format," unpublished paper

101. IBM Press Release (2001), "IBM's Test-Tube Quantum Computer Makes History," http://www.research.ibm.com/resources/news/20011219_quantum.shtml

102. Jahn, R. G. and Dunne, B. J. (1987), Margins of Reality: The Role of Consciousness in the Physical World, Harcourt Brace Jovanovich, New York

103. Jammer, M. (1974), <u>The Philosophy of Quantum Mechanics</u>, Wiley-Interscience, New York, pp. 507-521

104. Jennewein, T., Simon, C., Weihs, G., Weinfurter, H. and Zeilinger, A. (2000), "Quantum Cryptography with Entangled Photons," Phys. Rev. Lett., <u>84</u>, 4729-4732

105. Jinggen, H., Xinghai, Y. and Laijing, S. (1990), "Investigation into the 'Force' in Parapsychological Writing," Chinese J. Somatic Sci., <u>First Issue</u>, 32 [translated into English by the Defense Intelligence Agency]

106. Julsgaard, B., Kozhekin, A. and Polzik, E. S. (2001), "Experimental long-lived entanglement of two macroscopic objects," Nature, <u>413</u>, 400-403

107. Kaku, M. (1994), <u>Hyperspace: A Scientific Odyssey Through Parallel Universes, Time Warps, and the 10th Dimension</u>, Anchor Books-Doubleday, New York

108. Kaku, M. (1993), <u>Quantum Field Theory</u>, Oxford University Press, New York

109. Kaku, M. (1988), <u>Introduction to Superstrings</u>, Springer-Verlag, New York

110. Kaluza, T. (1921), "Unitätsproblem der Physik," Sitz. Preuss. Akad. Wiss. Phys. Math., <u>K1</u>, 966

111. Kaplan, A. E. and Ding, Y. J. (2000), "Field-gradient-induced second-harmonic generation in magnetized vacuum," Phys. Rev. A, <u>62</u>, 043805-(1-9)

112. Kim, Y.-H., Kulik, S. P. and Shih, Y. (2001), "Quantum Teleportation of a Polarization State with a Complete Bell State Measurement," Phys. Rev. Lett., <u>86</u>, 1370-1373

113. Klein, O. (1926), "Quantentheorie und fünfdimensionale Relativitätstheorie," Zeits. Phys., <u>37</u>, 895

114. Kongzhi, S., Xianggao, L. and Liangzhong, Z. (1990), "Research into Paranormal Ability to Break Through Spatial Barriers," Chinese J. Somatic Sci., <u>First Issue</u>, 22 [translated into English by the Defense Intelligence Agency]

115. Kuhn, T. S. (1970), <u>The Structure of Scientific Revolutions</u>, 2nd ed., Univ. of Chicago Press, Chicago

116. Kwiat, P. G., et al. (1995), "New high-intensity source of polarization-entangled photon pairs," Phys. Rev. Lett., <u>75</u>, 4337-4341

117. Kwiat, P. G., et al. (1999), "Ultrabright source of polarization-entangled photons," Phys. Rev. A., <u>60</u>, R773-R776

118. Lamas-Linares, A., Howell, J. C. and Bouwmeester, D. (2001), "Stimulated emission of polarization-entangled photons," Nature, <u>412</u>, 887-890

119. Lamoreaux, S. K. (1997), "Measurement of the Casimir Force Between Conducting Plates," Phys. Rev. Letters, <u>78</u>, 5-8

120. LaMothe, Capt. J. D. (1972), <u>Controlled Offensive Behavior – USSR</u>, Defense Intelligence Agency, Report No. ST-CS-01-169-72, DIA Task No. T72-01-14, Washington DC

121. Latorre, J. I., Pascual, P. and Tarrach, R. (1995), "Speed of light in non-trivial vacua," Nucl. Phys. B, <u>437</u>, 60-82

122. Lee, H. C. ed. (1984), <u>An Introduction to Kaluza-Klein Theories, Proc. Chalk River Workshop on Kaluza-Klein Theories</u>, World Scientific, Singapore

123. Lee, T. D. (1988), <u>Particle Physics and Introduction to Field Theory</u>, Harwood Academic Press, London

124. Leggett, A. J. (1999), "Quantum Theory: Weird and Wonderful," Physics World, <u>12</u>, 73-77

125. Leshan, C. (2002), "Proposal for Teleportation by Help of Vacuum Holes," in <u>Gravitation and Cosmology: From the Hubble Radius to the Planck Scale, Proc. of a Symposium in Honour of the 80th Birthday of Jean-Pierre Vigier</u>, Amoroso, R. L., Hunter, G., Kafatos, M. and Vigier, J.-P. eds., Kluwer Academic Publ., Boston, pp. 515-516

126. Leshan, C. (1999), "Thought Experiment to the Border of Universe," J. Theoretics, <u>1</u>, no.4

127. Li, L.-X. and Gott, J. R. (1998), "Self-Consistent Vacuum for Misner Space and the Chronology Protection Conjecture," Phys. Rev. Lett., <u>80</u>, 2980-2983

128. Lightman, A. P. and Gingerich, O. (1991), "When Do Anomalies Begin?," Science, <u>255</u>, 690-695

129. Lightman, A. P. and Lee, D. L. (1973), "Restricted proof that the weak equivalence principle implies the Einstein equivalence principle," Phys. Rev. D, 8, 364

130. Maierle, C., Lidar, D. and Harris, R. (1998), "How to teleport superpositions of chiral amplitudes," Phys. Rev. Lett., 81, 869-872

131. Maire, L. F. and LaMothe, Capt. J. D. (1975), Soviet and Czechoslovakian Parapsychology Research, Defense Intelligence Agency, Report No. DST-1810S-387-75, DIA Task No. PT-1810-12-75, Washington DC

132. Mandel, L. and Wolf, E. (1995), Optical Coherence and Quantum Optics, Cambridge University Press

133. Manning, H. P. (1977), The Fourth Dimension Simply Explained, Peter Smith Publ., Gloucester, MA

134. Mavromatos, N. E., Mershin, A. and Nanopoulos, D. V. (2002), "QED-Cavity model of microtubules implies dissipationless energy transfer and biological quantum teleportation," http://arxiv.org/abs/quant-ph/0204021

135. McConnell, A. J. (1957), Applications of Tensor Analysis, Dover Publ., New York, pp. 163-217

136. Mead, F. B. and Nachamkin, J. (1996), "System for Converting Electromagnetic Radiation Energy to Electrical Energy," United States Patent No. 5,590,031

137. Milonni, P. W. (1994), The Quantum Vacuum: An Introduction to Quantum Electronics, Academic Press, NY

138. Mitchell, E. D. (1999), "Nature's Mind: the Quantum Hologram," National Institute for Discovery Science, Las Vegas, NV, http://www.nidsci.org/articles/naturesmind-qh.html

139. Mitchell, E. D. (1974a), "Appendix: Experiments with Uri Geller," in Psychic Exploration: A Challenge for Science, Mitchell, E. D., White, J. ed., G. P. Putnam's Sons, New York, pp. 683-686

140. Mitchell, E. D. (1974b), Psychic Exploration: A Challenge for Science, White, J. ed., G. P. Putnam's Sons, New York

141. Mittelstaedt, P. (2000), "What if there are superluminal signals?," Eur. Phys. J. B, 13, 353-355

142. Mittelstaedt, P. (1998), "Can EPR-correlations be used for the transmission of superluminal signals?," Annalen der Physik, 7(7-8), 710-715

143. Mittelstaedt, P. and Nimtz, G. eds. (1998), "Workshop on Superluminal Velocities," Annalen der Physik, 7(7-8), 591-592

144. Morris, M. S. and Thorne, K. S. (1988), "Wormholes in spacetime and their use for interstellar travel: A tool for teaching general relativity", Am. J. Phys., 56, 395-412

145. Mourou, G. A., Barty, C. P. J. and Perry, M. D. (1998), "Ultrahigh-Intensity Lasers: Physics Of The Extreme On A Tabletop," Physics Today, 51, 22-28

146. Naik, D. S., Peterson, C. G., White, A. G., Berglund, A. J. and Kwiat, P. G. (2000), "Entangled state quantum cryptography: Eavesdropping on the Ekert protocol," Phys. Rev. Lett., 84, 4733

147. Nash, C. B. (1978), Science of PSI: ESP and PK, C. C. Thomas Publ., Springfield, Ill.

148. Nielsen, M. A. (2003), "Simple Rules for a Complex Quantum World," Sci. Am., 13, 25-33

149. Nielsen, M. A. and Chuang, I. L. (2000), Quantum Computation and Quantum Information, Cambridge University Press

150. Nielsen, M., Knill, E. and Laflamme, R. (1998), "Complete quantum teleportation using nuclear magnetic resonance," Nature, 396, 52-55

151. Nimtz, G. (1998), "Superluminal signal velocities," Annalen der Physik, 7(7-8), 618-624

152. Opatrný, T., Clausen, J., Welsch, D.-G. and Kurizki, G. (2000), "Squeezed-Vacuum Assisted Quantum Teleportation," Paper No. 7thCEWQO/015, in Proc. 7th Central-European Workshop on Quantum Optics, Hungary

153. Opatrný, T. and Kurizki, G. (2001), "Matter-Wave Entanglement and Teleportation by Molecular Dissociation and Collisions," Phys. Rev. Lett., 86, 3180-3183

154. Overduin, J. M. and Wesson, P. S. (1998), "Kaluza-Klein Gravity," http://arxiv.org/abs/gr-qc/9805018

155. Pan, J.-W., et al. (1998), "Experimental entanglement swapping," Phys. Rev. Lett., 80, 3891-3894

156. Pease, R. (2001), "Brane new world," Nature, 411, 986-988

157. Peres, A. (2000), "Classical intervention in quantum systems. II. Relativistic invariance," Phys. Rev. A, 61, 022117(8)

158. Perry, M. D. (2000), "The Amazing Power of the Petawatt," Science & Technology Rev. (LLNL-DoE publication), March issue, 4-12

159. Perry, M. D. (1996), "Crossing the Petawatt Threshold," Science & Technology Rev. (LLNL-DoE publication), December issue, 4-11

160. Polchinski, J. (1995), "Dirichlet Branes and Ramond-Ramond Charges," Phys. Rev. Lett., 75, 4724-4727

161. Pratt, J. G. (1986), "Soviet Research in Parapsychology," in Handbook of Parapsychology, Wolman, B. B., Dale, L. A., Schmeidler, G. R. and Ullman, M. eds., McFarland and Co. Publ., Jefferson, NC, pp. 883-903

162. Preskill, J., Lecture Notes: http://www.theory.caltech.edu/people/preskill/ph229/

163. Puthoff, H. E. (2003), Personal Communication, Institute for Advanced Studies at Austin, Austin, TX

164. Puthoff, H. E. (2002a), "Polarizable-Vacuum (PV) Approach to General Relativity", Found. Phys., 32, 927-943

165. Puthoff, H. E. (2002b), "Polarizable-Vacuum Approach to General Relativity", in Gravitation and Cosmology: From the Hubble Radius to the Planck Scale, eds. R. L. Amoroso, G. Hunter, M. Kafatos, and J.-P. Vigier, Kluwer Academic Publ., Dordrecht, the Netherlands, pp. 431-446

166. Puthoff, H. E. (1999a), "Polarizable-vacuum (PV) representation of general relativity," http://arxiv.org/abs/gr-qc/9909037

167. Puthoff, H. E. (1999b), Personal Communication, Institute for Advanced Studies at Austin, Austin, TX

168. Puthoff, H. E. (1996), "CIA-Initiated Remote Viewing Program at Stanford Research Institute," J. Sci. Explor., 10, 63-76

169. Puthoff, H. E. (1993), "On the Feasibility of Converting Vacuum Electromagnetic Energy to Useful Form," Int'l Workshop on the Zeropoint Electromagnetic Field, Cuernavaca, Mexico

170. Puthoff, H. E. (1990), "The Energetic Vacuum: Implications for Energy Research," Spec. in Sci. & Technology, 13, 247

171. Puthoff, H. E., Little, S. R. and Ibison, M. (2002), "Engineering the Zero-Point Field and Polarizable Vacuum for Interstellar Flight," J. British Interplanetary Soc., 55, 137-144

172. Puthoff, H. E. and Targ, R. (1975), "Physics, Entropy and Psychokinesis," in Proc. Conf. Quantum Physics and Parapsychology (Geneva, Switz.), Parapsychology Foundation Publ., New York

173. Puthoff, H. E. and Targ, R. (1974), "PK experiments with Uri Geller and Ingo Swann," in Research in Parapsychology 1973, Roll, W. G., Morris, R. L. and Morris, J. D. eds., Scarecrow Press, Metuchen, New Jersey, pp. 125-128

174. Quantum Information: Special Issue (1998), Physics World, 11, no. 3

175. Radin, D. (1997), The Conscious Universe: The Scientific Truth of Psychic Phenomena, HarperEdge-HarperCollins Publ., New York

176. Raimond, J. M., Brune, M. and Haroche, S. (2001), "Colloquium: Manipulating quantum entanglement with atoms and photons in a cavity," Rev. Mod. Phys., 73, 565-582

177. Randall, L. and Sundrum, R. (1999a), "Large Mass Hierarchy from a Small Extra Dimension," Phys. Rev. Lett., 83, 3370-3373

178. Randall, L. and Sundrum, R. (1999b), "An Alternative to Compactification," Phys. Rev. Lett., 83, 4690-4693

179. Rarity, J. G. (2003), "Getting Entangled in Free Space," Science, 301, 604 - 605

180. Reichenbach, H. (1957), The Philosophy of Space and Time, Dover Publ., New York

181. Rhine, L. E. (1970), Mind over Matter: Psychokinesis, Macmillan, New York

182. Rubakov, V. A. and Shaposhnikov, M. E. (1983a), "Do we live inside a domain wall?," Phys. Lett. B, 125, 136-138

183. Rubakov, V. A. and Shaposhnikov, M. E. (1983b), "Extra space-time dimensions: Towards a solution to the cosmological constant problem," Phys. Lett. B, 125, 139-143

184. Rucker, R. (1984), The Fourth Dimension: A Guided Tour of the Higher Universes, Houghton Mifflin Co., Boston, pp. 45-49

185. Rucker, R. (1977), Geometry, Relativity and the Fourth Dimension, Dover Publ., New York

186. Sackett, C. A. (2001), Quant. Inf. Comput., 1, 57

187. Sackett, C. A., et al. (2000), "Experimental entanglement of four particles," Nature, 404, 256

188. Scarani, V., Tittel, W., Zbinden, H. and Gisin, N. (2000), "The speed of quantum information and the preferred frame: analysis of experimental data," Phys. Lett. A, 276, 1-7

189. Scharnhorst, K. (1990), "On Propagation of Light in the Vacuum Between Plates," Phys. Lett. B, 236, 354-359

190. Schein, F. and Aichelburg, P. C. (1996), "Traversable Wormholes in Geometries of Charged Shells," Phys. Rev. Letters, 77, 4130-4133

191. Schmidt, H. (1987), "The Strange Properties of Psychokinesis," J. Sci. Explor., 1, no. 2

192. Schmidt, H. (1974), "Psychokinesis," in Psychic Exploration: A Challenge for Science, Mitchell, E. D., White, J. ed., G. P. Putnam's Sons, New York, pp. 179-193

193. Schnabel, J. (1997), Remote Viewers: The Secret History of America's Psychic Spies, Dell Publ., New York

194. Schrödinger, E. (1980), Proc. Am. Philos. Soc., 124, 323

195. Schrödinger, E. (1935a), Die Naturwissenschaften, 48, 807

196. Schrödinger, E. (1935b), Die Naturwissenschaften, 49, 823

197. Schrödinger, E. (1935c), Die Naturwissenschaften, 49, 844

198. Seife, C. (2000), "'Spooky Action' Passes a Relativistic Test," Science, 287, 1909-1910

199. Shan, G. (2003), "A Primary Quantum Model of Telepathy," http://cogprints.ecs.soton.ac.uk/archive/00003065/

200. Shigemi, S., Yasuo, O. and Akihira, T. (1978), "Some Observations with Scanning Electron Microscope (SEM) of the Fracture Surface of Metals Fractured by Psychokinesis," Japan PS Soc. J., 2, no. 2

201. Shor, P. W. (1997), "Polynomial-Time Algorithms for Prime Factorization and Discrete Logarithms on a Quantum Computer," SIAM J. Sci. Statist. Comput., 26, 1484

202. Shor, P. W. (1994), "Polynomial-Time Algorithms for Prime Factorization and Discrete Logarithms on a Quantum Computer", in Proc. 35th Annual Symposium on Foundations of Computer Science, IEEE Computer Society Press, p. 124

203. Shoup, R. (2002), "Anomalies and Constraints: Can Clairvoyance, Precognition, and Psychokinesis Be Accommodated within Known Physics?," J. Sci. Explor., 16, no. 1

204. Shuhuang, L., et al. (1981), "Some Experiments on the Transfer of Objects Performed by Unusual Abilities of the Human Body," Nature Journal (Peoples Republic of China), 4, no. 9, 652 [Defense Intelligence Agency Requirements and Validation Branch, DIA Translation LN731-83, Intelligence Information Report No. 6010511683 (1983)]

205. Siegfried, T. (2000), The Bit and the Pendulum, John Wiley & Sons

206. Sørensen, J. L. (1998), Nonclassical light for atomic physics and quantum teleportation, Ph.D. thesis, Univ. of Aarhus

207. Srikanth, R. (July 1999), "Noncausal superluminal nonlocal signaling," http://arxiv.org/abs/quant-ph/9904075

208. Stanford, R. (1974), "Interview," Psychic, 7

209. Stenholm, S. and Bardroff, P. (1998), "Teleportation of N-dimensional states," Phys. Rev. A, 58, 4373-4376

TELEPORTATION

210. Swann, I. (1974), "Scientological Techniques: A Modern Paradigm for the Exploration of Consciousness and Psychic Integration," in Proc. First Int'l Conf. on Psychotronic Research, United States Joint Publications Research Service, Document No. JPRS L/5022-1, Virginia

211. Targ, R. (1996), "Remote Viewing at Stanford Research Institute in the 1970s: A Memoir," J. Sci. Explor., 10, 77-88

212. Targ, R. and Puthoff, H. E. (1977), Mind-Reach: Scientists Look at Psychic Ability, Jonathan Cape Ltd.-Anchor Press, London

213. Tart, C. T., Puthoff, H. E. and Targ, R. eds. (2002), Mind at Large: Institute of Electrical and Electronics Engineers Symposia on the Nature of Extrasensory Perception, Hampton Roads Publ. Co., Charlottesville, VA

214. Terhal, B. M., Wolf, M. M. and Doherty, A. C. (2003), "Quantum Entanglement: A Modern Perspective," Physics Today, 56, 46-52

215. Thorne, K. S. (1993), "Closed Timelike Curves," GRP-340, CalTech, Pasadena, CA

216. Tittel, W. and Weihs, G. (2001), Quantum Inf. Comput., 1, 3

217. Tittel, W., Brendel, J., Zbinden, H. and Gisin, N. (2000), "Quantum Cryptography Using Entangled Photons in Energy-Time Bell States," Phys. Rev. Lett., 84, 4737-4740

218. Tittel, W., Brendel, J., Gisin, B., Herzog, T., Zbinden, H. and Gisin, N. (1998a), "Experimental demonstration of quantum correlations over more than 10 km," Phys. Rev. A, 57, 3229-3232

219. Tittel, W., Brendel, J., Zbinden, H. and Gisin, N. (1998b), "Violation of Bell Inequalities by Photons More Than 10 km Apart," Phys. Rev. Lett., 81, 3563-3566

220. Vaidman, L. (1994), "Teleportation of quantum states," Phys. Rev. A, 49, 1473-1476

221. Vaidman, L. and Yoran, N. (1999), "Methods for reliable teleportation," Phys. Rev. A, 59, 116-125

222. Vallee, J. (1997), Personal Communication, Science Advisory Board of the National Institute for Discovery Science, Las Vegas, NV

223. Vallee, J. (1990), Confrontations: A Scientist's Search for Alien Contact, Ballantine Books, New York

224. Vallee, J. (1988), Dimensions: A Casebook of Alien Contact, Ballantine Books, New York

225. van Enk, S. (March 1998), "No-cloning and superluminal signaling," http://arxiv.org/abs/quant-ph/9803030

226. Visser, M., Kar, S. and Dadhich, N. (2003), "Traversable Wormholes with Arbitrarily Small Energy Condition Violations," Phys. Rev. Lett., 90, 201102

227. Visser, M. (1997), Personal Communication, Washington University, St. Louis, MO

228. Visser, M. (1995), Lorentzian Wormholes: From Einstein to Hawking, AIP Press, New York

229. Visser, M. (1990), "Wormholes, baby universes, and causality", Phys. Rev. D, 41, 1116-1124

230. Visser, M. (1989), "Traversable wormholes: Some simple examples", Phys. Rev. D, 39, 3182-3184

231. Volkov, A. M., Izmest'ev, A. A. and Skrotskii, G. V. (1971), "The propagation of electromagnetic waves in a Riemannian space," Sov. Phys. JETP, 32, 686-689

232. Walker, E. H. (1974), "Consciousness and Quantum Theory," in Psychic Exploration: A Challenge for Science, Mitchell, E. D., White, J. ed., G. P. Putnam's Sons, New York, pp. 544-568

233. Weihs, G., Jennewein, T., Simon, C., Weinfurter, H. and Zeilinger, A. (1998), "Violation of Bell's Inequality under Strict Einstein Locality Conditions," Phys. Rev. Lett., 81, 5039-5043

234. Weinberg, S. (1992), Dreams of a Final Theory, Vintage Books, pp. 88-89

235. Weinberg, S. (1989), "Testing Quantum Mechanics," Ann. Phys., 194, 336-386

236. Weiss, P. (2000), "Hunting for Higher Dimensions: Experimenters scurry to test new theories suggesting that extra dimensions are detectable," Science News, 157, 122-124

237. Westmoreland, M. and Schumacher, B. (March 1998), "Quantum entanglement and the non existence of superluminal signals," http://arxiv.org/abs/quant-ph/9801014

238. Wheeler, J. A. (1962), Monist, 47, 40

239. Wheeler, J. A. (1957), Rev. Mod. Phys., <u>29</u>, 463

240. Wheeler, J. A. and Zurek, W. H. eds. (1983), <u>Quantum Theory and Measurement</u>, Princeton University Press

241. Will, C. M. (1993), <u>Theory and Experiment in Gravitational Physics</u> (rev. ed.), Cambridge University Press, Cambridge, Section 2.6

242. Will, C. M. (1989), "The confrontation between gravitation theory and experiment," in <u>General Relativity: An Einstein Centenary Survey</u>, eds. S. W. Hawking and W. Israel, Cambridge University Press, Cambridge, Chapter 2

243. Will, C. M. (1974), "Gravitational red-shift measurements as tests of nonmetric theories of gravity," Phys. Rev. D, <u>10</u>, 2330-2337

244. Wilson, H. A. (1921), "An electromagnetic theory of gravitation," Phys. Rev., <u>17</u>, 54-59

245. Wineland, D. J., et al. (2002), "Quantum information processing with trapped ions," http://arxiv.org/abs/quant-ph/0212079

246. Wolf, F. A. (1988), <u>Parallel Universes: The Search for Other Worlds</u>, Simon and Schuster, New York

247. Wolman, B. B., Dale, L. A., Schmeidler, G. R. and Ullman, M. eds. (1986), <u>Handbook of Parapsychology</u>, McFarland and Co. Publ., Jefferson, NC

248. Wootters, W. K. and Zurek, W. H. (1982), "A single quantum cannot be cloned," Nature, <u>299</u>, 802-803

249. Zbinden, H., Brendel, J., Gisin, N. and Tittel, W. (2000a), "Experimental Test of Non-Local Quantum Correlation in Relativistic Configurations," http://arxiv.org/abs/quant-ph/0007009

250. Zbinden, H., Brendel, J., Tittel, W. and Gisin, N. (2000b), "Experimental Test of Relativistic Quantum State Collapse with Moving Reference Frames," http://arxiv.org/abs/quant-ph/0002031

251. Zeilinger, A. (2003), "Quantum Teleportation," Sci. Am, <u>13</u>, 34-43

252. Zhang, T. C., et al. (2002), "Quantum teleportation of light beams," http://arxiv.org/abs/quant-ph/0207076

253. Zubairy, S. (1998), "Quantum teleportation of a field state," Phys. Rev. A, <u>58</u>, 4368-4372

TELEPORTATION

APPENDIX A – A Few Words About Negative Energy

A.1 A General Relativistic Definition of Negative or Exotic Energy

We saw in equations (2.10a-c) that the surface energy and stress-tension densities of the material required to create and thread a traversable wormhole must be "negative." For surface stress-energy, and volume stress-energy in general, this is "negative" in the sense that the material we must deploy to generate and thread the traversable wormhole must have an energy density (ρc^2, ρ = mass density) that is less than the stress-energy density (τ), or we can write this condition as: *mass-energy* $\rho c^2 \leq$ *stress-energy* τ. On the basis of this condition, we call this material property "exotic." Therefore, the term "negative" is just a misnomer in this context. The condition for ordinary, non-exotic forms of matter that we are all familiar with is *mass-energy* $\rho c^2 >$ *stress-energy* τ. This condition represents one version of what is variously called the weak (WEC), null (NEC), average (AEC), dominant (DEC), strong (SEC) or "standard" energy conditions (that are mere hypotheses!), which allegedly forbid negative mass-energy density and gravitational repulsion (antigravity) between material objects to occur in nature. Hawking and Ellis (1973) formulated these energy conditions in order to establish a series of mathematical proofs in their study of the application of general relativity theory to cosmology and black hole physics.

However, there are general theorems of differential geometry that guarantee that there must be NEC violations (meaning exotic matter-energy is present) at a wormhole throat (Visser, 1997). In view of this, it is known that static radial electric or magnetic fields are borderline exotic when threading a wormhole, if their tension were infinitesimally larger, for a given energy density (Herrmann, 1989; Hawking and Ellis, 1973). Other exotic (energy condition violating) matter-energy fields are known to be squeezed quantum states of the electromagnetic field and other squeezed quantum fields (see Section A.2 for the discussion on squeezed quantum states), gravitationally squeezed vacuum electromagnetic zero-point energy (see Section 2.3 for the discussion on Gravitationally Squeezed Vacuum Energy), Casimir (electromagnetic zero-point) energy and other quantum fields/states/effects. These examples represent forms of matter-energy that possess negative energy density. Since the vacuum is defined to have vanishing energy density, anything possessing less energy density than the vacuum must have a negative energy density. With respect to creating wormholes, these have the unfortunate reputation of alarming physicists. This is unfounded since all the energy condition hypotheses have been experimentally tested in the laboratory and experimentally shown to be false - 25 years before their formulation (Visser, 1990 and references cited therein). Further investigation into this technical issue showed that violations of the energy conditions are widespread for all forms of both classical and quantum matter-energy such as planets, stars, black holes, neutron stars, people, space dust clouds, etc. (Davis, 1999b; Barcelo and Visser, 2002). In addition, Visser (1995) showed that all (generic) spacetime geometries violate all the energy conditions. Violating the energy conditions commits no offense against nature.

A.2 Squeezed Quantum States and Negative Energy

In quantum mechanics the energy (E) and frequency (ν) of a quantum oscillator system, such as electromagnetic radiation (or light), are interchangeable via the Planck relation $E = h\nu$ ($h = 2\pi\hbar$). And from the Heisenberg quantum uncertainty principle, we know that the conjugate variable to the frequency is the oscillator phase (φ), such that $\Delta\nu\Delta\varphi \geq \hbar$ is obeyed. Phase is difficult to measure and is ignored in characterizing complex quantum systems.

Recent theoretical and experimental work has shown that in many quantum systems the limits to measurement precision imposed by the quantum vacuum zero-point fluctuations (ZPF) can be breached by decreasing the frequency noise at the expense of increasing the phase noise (thus maintaining $\Delta\nu\Delta\varphi \geq \hbar$), while at the same time the variations in frequency, and therefore the energy, are reduced below the ZPF such that the energy becomes "negative." "Squeezing" is thus the control of quantum fluctuations and corresponding uncertainties, whereby one can squeeze the variance of one (physically important) observable quantity provided the variance in the (physically unimportant) conjugate variable is stretched/increased. The squeezed quantity possesses an unusually low variance, meaning less variance than would be expected on the basis of the equipartition theorem. We can exploit quantum squeezing to extract energy from one place in the ordinary vacuum at the expense of piling up excess energy elsewhere (Morris and Thorne, 1988).

TELEPORTATION

Appendix B – *TH*εμ Methodology

In the formalism of the *TH*εμ methodology, the functions T and H are introduced by requiring that the Lagrangian for the motion of particles (with charge e_a and mass m_{0a} for the ath particle), under the joint action of gravity and the electromagnetic field A_α ($\alpha \equiv$ spacetime vector components), be expressed in the canonical form

$$L = \sum_a \int \left(-m_{0a} \sqrt{T - H v_a^2} + e_a A_\alpha v_a^{\alpha} \right) dt + \left(8\pi \right)^{-1} \int \left(\varepsilon \mathbf{E}^2 + \mu^{-1} \mathbf{B}^2 \right) d^3x \, dt \qquad \text{(B.1)};$$

where the arbitrary functions T, H, ε, and μ are functions of the metric (a.k.a. gravitation field), v_a^{α} is the ath particle four-vector velocity, and A_α is the electromagnetic field four-vector potential, $\mathbf{E}$ and $\mathbf{B}$ are the electric and magnetic field strengths, and (B.1) is in geometrodynamic natural units ($\hbar = c_0 = G = \varepsilon_0 = \mu_0 = 1$). The Lagrangian characterizes the motion of charged particles in an external gravitational field by the two functions T and H, and characterizes the response of the electromagnetic fields to the external gravitational field by the two functions ε and μ. For all standard (metric) theories of gravity, the four functions are related by

$$\varepsilon = \mu = \sqrt{\frac{H}{T}} \qquad \text{(B.2)};$$

and *every* metric theory of gravity satisfies this relation, such that the Einstein Equivalence Principle is satisfied.

TELEPORTATION

AFRL-PR-ED-TR-2003-0034
Primary Distribution of this Report:

AFRL/PRSP (15 CD)
Dr. Frank Mead
10 E. Saturn Blvd
Edwards AFB CA 93524-7680

AFRL/PRSA (1 CD)
Dr. Jean-Luc Cambier
10 E. Saturn Blvd.
Edwards AFB CA 93524-7680

AFRL/PR (1 CD)
Dr. Alan Garscadden
1950 Fifth Street
Building 18
Wright-Patterson AFB, OH 45433-7251

AFRL/PR Technical Library (2 CD + 1 HC)
6 Draco Drive
Edwards AFB CA 93524-7130

Chemical Propulsion Information Agency (1 CD)
Attn: Tech Lib (Dottie Becker)
10630 Little Patuxent Parkway, Suite 202
Columbia MD 21044-3200

Defense Technical Information Center
(1 Electronic Submission via STINT)
Attn: DTIC-ACQS (Pat Mawby)
8725 John J. Kingman Road, Suite 94
Ft. Belvoir VA 22060-6218

Dr. Eric Davis (10 CD)
4849 San Rafael Ave.
Las Vegas, NV 89120

Dr. Dana Andrews (1 CD)
P.O. Box 36
Leavenworth, WA 98826

Dr. Jim Degnan (1 CD)
AFRL/DEHP
Kirtland AFB, NM 87117

Dr. Greg Benford (1 CD)
Physics Department
University of California
Irvine, CA 92717

Dr. Jim Benford (1 CD)
Microwave Sciences, Inc.
1041 Los Arabis Ln.
Lafayette, CA 94549

Dr. Gary L. Bennett (1 CD)
7517 West Devonwood Dr.
Boise, ID 83703

Dr. Mitat Birkan (1 CD)
AFOSR/NA
801 N. Randolf St.
Arlington, VA 22203

Dr. Jon Campbell (1 CD)
P.O. Box 295
Harvest, AL 35749

Mr. Michael Libeau
NSWCDD
17320 Dahlgren Rd.
Attn: Code G23 Libeau
Dalgren VA 22448

Dr. Phil Carpenter (1 CD)
US Dept. of Energy
Oak Ridge National Laboratory
P.O. Box 2008, MS: 6269
Oak Ridge, TN 37831

Dr. Brice N. Cassenti (1 CD)
Pratt & Whitney Aircraft
400 Main Street – MS: 163-07
East Hartford, CT 06108

Dr. Chan K. Choi (1 CD)
Purdue University
School of Nuclear Engineering
West Lafayette, IN 47907

Dr. Terry Kammash (1 CD)
University of Michigan
Nuclear Engineering Dept.
Ann Arbor, MI 48109

76

Dr. Ingrid Wysong (1 CD)
EOARD
223-321-Old Merylebone Rd.
London NW1 5th
United Kingdom

Dr. Robert Frisbee (1 CD)
JPL, MS 125-109
4800 Oak Grove Dr.
Pasadena, CA 91109

Dave Froning (1 CD)
Flight Unlimited
5450 Country Club
Flagstaff, AZ 86004

Geroge D. Hathaway (1 CD)
Hathaway Consulting Services
39 Kendal Ave.
Toronto, Canada, Ontario
Canada M5R 1L5

Clark W. Hawk, Director (1 CD)
Propulsion Research Center
University of Alabama in Huntsville
5000 Technology Drive, TH S-266
Huntsville, AL 35899

Alan C. Holt (1 CD)
NASA/Johnson Space Center
Code OD
Houston, TX 77058

Dr. Steven Howe (1 CD)
19 Karen Lane
Los Alamos, NM 87544

Mike Kaiserman (1 CD)
Raytheon Missile Systems Company
Bldg 805, M/S C3
Tucson, AZ 85734

Dr. George Miley (1 CD)
University of Illinois, Dept. of Nuclear Engr.
214 Nuclear Engineering Laboratory
103 South Goodwin Ave.
Urbana, IL 61801

Marc Millis (1 CD)
NASA Glenn Research Center
M.S. SPTD-2
21000 Brookpark Road, MS: 86-2
Cleveland, OH 44135

Dr. Jordon Kare (1 CD)
222 Canyon Lakes Pl.
San Ramon, CA 94583

Ron J. Kita (1 CD)
87 Shady Springs DR.
Doyelstown, PA 18901

Dr. Gerald L. Kulcinski (1 CD)
Nuclear Engineering Dept.
University of Wisconsin
1500 Johnson Dr.
Madison, WI 53706

Dr. Geoffrey A. Landis (1 CD)
Sverdrup Technology
21000 Brookpark Rd., MS 302-1
Cleveland, OH 44135

Dr. Michael LaPointe (1 CD)
NASA Lewis Research Center, MS: SPTD-1
21000 Brookpark Rd.
Cleveland, OH 44135

Dr. Sheldon Meth (1 CD)
DARPA
Tactical Technology Office
3701 N. Fairfax Dr.
Arlington, VA 22203

Dr. Michael M. Micci (1 CD)
Prof. of Aerospace Engineering
233 E. Hammond Bldg.
University Park, PA 16802

Dr. Hal Puthoff (1 CD)
Institute for Advanced Studies
4030 Braker Lane, West
Suite 300
Austin, TX 78759

Dr. Eric E. Rice (1 CD)
Orbital Technologies Corp.
402 Gammon Place, Suite 10
Madison, WI 53719

TELEPORTATION

Dr. Aurthur Morrish (1 CD)
DARPA/ATO
3701 N. Fairfax Dr.
Arlington, VA 22203

Dr. Paul Murad (1 CD)
Sr. Analyst, Director for Intel Production
Missile & Space Intel Center
Defense Intelligence Agency
Washington, DC 20340-6054

Dr. Brian Palaszewski (1 CD)
NASA Glenn Research Center
21000 Brookpartk Road, MS: 5-10
Cleveland, OH 44135

Dr. Alan Pike (1 CD)
DSAS
1988 Crescent Park Drive
Reston, VA 20190

Dr. Dennis Pelaccio (1 CD)
SAIC
8100 Shaffer Parkway, Suite 100
Littleton, CO 80127

Ben Plenge (1 CD)
101 W. Eglin Blvd
Suite 342
Eglin AFB, FL 32542-6810

Dr. James Powell (1 CD)
Plus Ultra Technologies, Inc.
25 East Loop Rd.
Stony Brook, NY 11970-3350

Mr. Charles A. Yost (1 CD)
Electric Spacecraft Journal
73 Sunlight Drive
Leicester, NC 28748

Dr. George Schmidt (1 CD)
NASA HQ
300 E. Street SW
Washington, DC 20546

Steve Squires (1 CD)
Directorate of Applied Technology
   Test and Simulation
STEWS-DATTS-OO
WSMR, NM 88002

Robert Talley (1 CD)
Topaz 2000, Inc
3380 Sheridan Dr.
Suite 172
Amherst, NY 14226

Dr. Kenneth D. Ware (1 CD)
Defense Nuclear Agency
Simulation Technology
6801 Telegraph Road
Alexandria, VA 22310

Dr. Feiedwardt Winterberg (1 CD)
University of Nevada
Desert Research Institute
Reno, NV 89507

Dr. Young Bae (1 CD)
1101 Bryan Ave.
Suite C
Tustin, CA 92780

Dr. Thomas M York (1 CD)
1215 Inverary Pl.
State College, PA 16801

Dr. Robert J. Barker (1CD)
AFOSR/NE
801 N. Randolf St.
Arlington, VA 22203

* 9 7 8 1 6 0 6 1 1 1 4 8 2 *